✺ INSIGHT   POCKET GUIDE

FIJI
ISLANDS

Discovery
CHANNEL

APA PUBLICATIONS   **L**
Part of the Langenscheidt Publishing Group

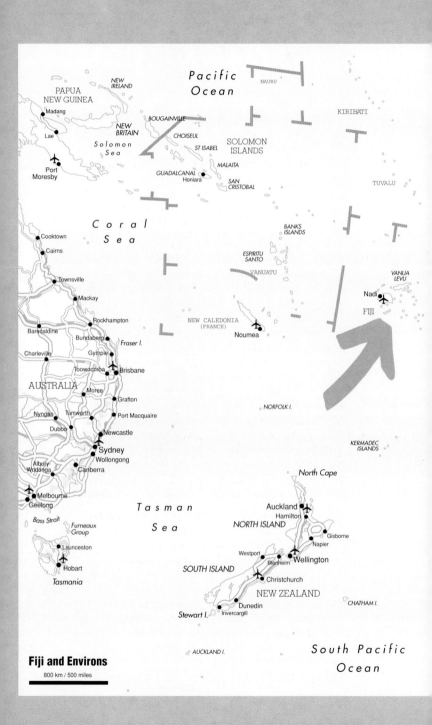

Fiji and Environs

800 km / 500 miles

Welcome!

This guidebook combines the interests and enthusiasms of two of the world's best-known information providers: Insight Guides, who have set the standard for visual travel guides since 1970, and Discovery Channel, the world's premier source of non-fiction television programming. Its aim is to bring you the best of the Fiji Islands in a series of itineraries devised by Insight's Fiji correspondent, James Siers.

Dazzling white-sand beaches, brilliant turquoise-blue waters, rustic villages and time-forgotten townships. Fiji's bejewelled islands offer all these and more. Three full-day itineraries in this guide quickly introduce you to the varied attractions on the main island of Viti Levu. A series of *Pick & Mix* options, in and outside Viti Levu, offer more leisurely diversions while those with more time can venture further afield with the *Excursions* section. Here are suggestions for visits to the outer islands, traditional villages, hikes to the jungle-clad interiors, stays at exclusive resorts and luxury cruises, as well as suggestions on diving, surfing, whitewater kayaking and deep-sea fishing trips. Select as few or as many of the itineraries as you wish. Together, they represent the best of what Fiji's more than 330 islands have to offer. Chapters on history and culture, eating out and nightlife, and a useful practical information section complete this reader-friendly guide.

 James Siers, writer, filmmaker and adventurer, first visited Fiji in 1962 while on a photo-journalism assignment. He was captivated by the striking scenery, the gracious people and Fiji's romantic past. 'In the 30 years since that first visit,' Siers recalls, 'I became a frequent visitor, to write and photograph several books on the islands as well as to direct films. After returning almost every year, in 1984, I decided this was the place I would sink my roots.'

C O N T E N T S

Pages 2/3:
Yachts at anchor,
Mamanuca Islands

Excursions

The following six excursions are ideal for visitors with more time. They range from two days to a week or more and cover a range of activities and a spectrum of Fijian islands.

Pages 8/9: Smiling Fijian youngsters

Activities, Shopping, Eating Out & Nightlife

Calendar of Special Events

Practical Information

Maps

HISTORY & CULTURE

Fiji's human history began sometime around the year 1500BC. There is no evidence as to who those first settlers were. Items unearthed in burial sites and archaeological excavations show that they were of the same stock as those who later became the Polynesians of Tonga, Samoa and the major islands of the east: Tahiti, Hawaii, the Marquesas, Tuamotus, Gambiers, Austral Islands, Easter Island and New Zealand.

Various theories postulate that the first settlers lived in Fiji for more than 1,000 years after its discovery, co-existing with later migrants in a state of war and peace. During this process, the people we recognise today as Polynesian gradually moved to eastern Fiji, the Lau Islands and Tonga, until finally, the Fijians, as we know them today, became dominant over the entire group of islands.

Point of Origin

The undoubted point of origin was Southeast Asia, which includes Indonesia, Philippines, Borneo and Papua New Guinea. Human habitation of New Guinea has now been established to have occurred more than 40,000 years ago. At a later date, new migrants began to move down and at some point, now thought to have been 5,000 years ago, a maritime culture established itself in New Ireland and New Britain and then quickly moved down through the Solomon Islands to Vanuatu, New Caledonia and Fiji and on to Tonga, Samoa, the Marquesas, Tahiti, Hawaii and New Zealand. This achievement ranks them as the greatest sailors the world has ever known.

Those early sailors who fearlessly roamed the Pacific Ocean are today referred to as the Lapita, because of a distinct style of pottery first discovered in 1952 at a site in New Caledonia of the same name. Pottery remains discovered in Marquesas tell an interesting story: the material used for grouting came from the Rewa River delta on Viti Levu island in Fiji. This points to trading links between the people of Tonga

A communal gathering outside a Fijian bure

Early bare-breasted Fijian beauties

and Fiji, and to active voyaging from Tonga to Samoa and the east.

Scientists working with the tools of archaeology, linguistics and botany are still trying to piece together what really might have happened but enough has been revealed to paint the following scenario: The Lapita discovered and settled in Fiji sometime before 1500BC. Within a short time of their settlement, some continue with exploratory voyages to Tonga, Samoa and then the major islands of east Polynesia.

The remaining population increases and war once again becomes endemic. New migrants arrive from the west and human bones are discovered in middens, along with those of animals and other food-stuffs. Cannibalism becomes part of life. Fiji enters a period of intense political rivalry which exists up to the time of European contact. Some aspects of Melanesian culture are retained but the material and social culture is principally Polynesian.

European Contact

In 1643, Dutch navigator Abel Tasman sailed to the north-east of Fiji. The reef which was nearly his ruin bears the name Heemskirk, after one of his ships. Tasman sighted the islands of Taveuni, Qamea, Laucala, Rabi and part of Vanua Levu, but he did not pause to examine his discovery. Captain James Cook was next in 1774. He anchored off the island of Vatoa in southern Lau, left some trinkets ashore and continued to the west without realising the extent of the archipelago.

The true extent of Fiji was not discovered until 1789 when Captain William Bligh sailed through the entire group after being set adrift in Tonga by the mutineers who seized the HMS *Bounty*. Bligh passed through a portion of Lau in eastern Fiji and then between Koro and Wakaya, within easy distance of Ovalau and through the Vatu i Ra channel which divides Viti Levu from Vanua Levu. He went on past Yasawa i Rara at the north-western extremity, thus leaving Fiji behind. A large canoe was launched by the Fijians in pursuit from Yasawa i Rara and came within bow shot of Bligh and his men. Several arrows were fired but Bligh and his men managed to escape.

As a result, the large, reef-strewn body of water between the north-western coast of Viti Levu, the Yasawa Islands and the Mamanutha Islands is to this day known as Bligh Water.

Cannibalism

Europeans who ventured to Fiji before the turn of the century confirmed stories told in Tonga of hazardous reefs and the duplicity of the people and their cannibal appetites. In 1794, the captain of the American brig *Arthur* had to defend his ship with musket and cannon against the natives. During the course of the next 50 years, less cautious captains would lose their vessels. These hazards were sufficient to deter casual traffic, but when sandalwood was discovered it offered sufficient incentive to overlook both the dangers. This period in Fiji's history began just after the end of the 18th century and ended some 10 years later but it was to have a profound effect on the Fijian people, and their culture and politics.

The most important effect was the introduction of the gun and its unscrupulous use by shipwrecked mercenaries, the most signifi-

Fijian outrigger canoe

cant of whom was Charlie Savage, a Swede. Coupled with the policy of an ambitious chief on the small island of Bau, the weapons proved decisive in war and helped elevate Bau to a state of pre-eminence which it enjoys to this day.

Savage was rewarded with many wives from well-born families; the male issue of whom were strangled at birth so as not to complicate future succession claims. He was regarded with dread and awe by most Fijians. His reputation, however, was not sufficient to save his life during a skirmish in Vanua Levu following a dispute. Savage, who went to parley with the opposing side, was drowned by having his head immersed in a pool of water and then dismembered, cooked and eaten before his friends. The episode ended less dramatically so for his friends: they managed to seize the head priest as hostage and were thus able to get to safety.

New Trade

Ten years after the demise of the sandalwood trade, a new trade began for *beche de mer* (sea cucumber) in the 1820s. As with sandalwood, a fortune could be made and this was enough to bring many ships to Fiji where they became embroiled in local conflicts. By now Fiji also had a resident population of European beachcombers.

Some like Charlie Savage were shipwrecked castaways; others had jumped ship; some like William Lockerby and David Whippy had been left on the beach because of conflict with their superior officers. Yet others came to seek their fortunes in trade.

The natural centre for these men was Levuka, on the island of Ovalau, where the prevailing east-south-east wind made it easy for sailing ships to enter and leave port. Levuka was also in close proximity to the centres of power at Bau and Rewa and the most populous parts of Fiji. Some of these men gained fortunes. The American David Whippy, whose descendants number more than 1,000 today, is a good example. Left ashore by his elder brother, he at first became a mercenary, rose to be trusted ambassador to the state of Bau and later became appointed the American consul for Fiji.

Later, he acquired 9,000 acres of land

13

Levuka – the old capital in the 19th century

at Wainunu in Vanua Levu, and established a shipyard (which until 1990 was operated by his descendants) and died an honoured man.

At the time of European contact, the relatively new state of Bau was on the ascent against its neighbours, the ancient and most powerful states of Verata and Rewa. Cakaudrove, which controlled a large part of Vanua Levu, Taveuni and its associated smaller islands, was also in contention but eventually, as did the others, acknowledged Bau as pre-eminent.

Conversion to Christianity

A new consideration was the arrival of Tongan chief Ma'afu in Fiji in 1840 who came close to winning control of the entire Fijian group. He was thwarted in his ambition by the cession of Fiji to Britain by leading chiefs in 1874. The importance of Wesleyan missionaries who arrived in 1835 from Tonga cannot be overlooked in this equation because it was the 1853 conversion of Seru Cakobau, the Vunivalu (chief) of Bau, and decisive Tongan intervention in a war between Cakobau and others which finally ended the chapter on old Fiji. Cakobau's conversion to Christianity also brought about the conversion of most of the population.

Cession to Britain

The inability of Cakobau to form an effective government in the 1870s caused a crisis of a magnitude which could not be resolved. The ever more threatening Tongan presence, directed by the able Ma'afu was poised to swallow Fiji as a colony of Tonga and gave added impetus for the Bauan chief and other leading chiefs to cede the islands to Britain in 1874.

The cession of Fiji encouraged a new wave of European settlers. A plantation society which grew and processed coconuts into oil was developed in the 1840s and began to thrive. Only the lack of cheap, reliable labour held it in check. A stop had been put to 'black birding' – a practice nothing short of slavery – just prior to cession. Islanders in the Solomons and Vanuatu had been lured aboard 'recruiting' ships with promises of trade goods and then abducted to be contracted to plantation owners in Fiji.

The planting and processing of sugar cane made it imperative to have a large supply of cheap labour and so the colonial administration decided to recruit indentured labour from India on 5-year contracts. The first contingent arrived in 1878 and the system was to continue until 1916. By this time, Fiji's sugar industry was controlled by the Australian Colonial Sugar Refining Company. As the company could not survive without the Indians, a government decision was made to allow those who wished to stay in Fiji to do so, despite protests from the Great Council of (Fijian) Chiefs. Most chose to remain and by 1970, when Fiji became independent, Indians outnumbered native Fijians in a total population of over 700,000.

Military Coups

In 1987, a coalition between the Indians and Fijians won the general election and provoked two (bloodless) military coups by the army, almost entirely composed of Fijian troops. A new constitution was promulgated which gave Fijians a guaranteed majority in government. In 1992, 5 years after the coups, a general election was held. The man who had engineered the coups, Major-General Sitiveni Rabuka, became the Prime Minister of a coalition comprising members of his own Fijian party sponsored by the chiefs and that of the general electors who represented people of European, part-European, Chinese, part-Chinese and of Pacific Island origin.

In 1997, in response to criticisms that the existing constitution was undemocratic and racially divisive, a new constitution was drafted, allowing for a multi-racial government. In May 1999, the elections returned a coalition led by the Fiji Labour Party (FLP) to victory and Fiji-Indian Mahendra Pal Chaudry became prime minister. This was met with protests by ethnic Fijians and sparked a series of explosions in Suva in August. In May 2000, Chaudry and FLP members were taken hostage in parliament for 56 days by coup leader George Speight and other armed gunmen. The coup failed, however, and Speight and his associates were arrested and eventually sentenced to 'life' in prison.

An interim government– which did not include members of Chaudry's ad-

Ratu Seru Cakobau

Fijian entertainment

ministration – was formed in July 2000 with Laisenia Qarase as prime minister. In the September 2001 general election, Qarase was returned as head of an indigenous Fijian coalition government. Qarase remains in power and new elections will take place around 2006.

Given the Indian dominance over the economy, it may be that Fijian politics will see further confrontation between its 51-percent-strong ethnic Fijian majority and its smaller 49-percent Indian population. The Fijian economy, already plagued with rising unemployment and a troubled sugar cane industry, has been hard hit by this recent spate of events, and will take a long time to recover.

Fijian Culture

About 90 percent of Fijians still live in villages in the countryside and the power of the *vanua* – one's land and family ties – is still the most powerful cultural force. Extended family units known as *matagali* comprise village communities who own land in common. The concept of individual ownership is foreign in a village where everything is shared and the word *kerekere* means a request that cannot be denied.

In practice, Fijians who live in cities and are faced with expenditure for rent, food and clothing find it difficult to cope with requests from relatives who arrive, expecting to be housed, fed and clothed without concern as to who will pay for it. The problem is magnified when a Fijian ventures into business. If he has a store and a distant relative without money wants to buy something, he cannot refuse, knowing full well the account will never be settled.

Each village has a chief who in turn owes allegiance to a higher chief. Paramount chiefs represent former political states and command the highest respect. They comprise the Bose Levu Vaka Turaga (Great Council of Chiefs) whose deliberations and decisions are held by some to be more important than those of parliament. These are men descended from the chiefs who ceded Fiji to Britain in 1874, and who now claim the right of their ancestors to supreme authority in independent Fiji.

The other half of Fiji's population comprises the descendants of Indian indentured labourers who began arriving in the country in 1878. By scraping and saving, and hard work and investment, some have prospered beyond belief. This is often a sore point with many Fijians who want to maintain political control until such time they have reached economic parity, a concept which many consider impossible to achieve without a cultural revolution.

Caught in a vicelike grip between keeping an old way of life and its traditions and trying to cope with rising expectations, the Fijian people are struggling to make adjustments to their way of life.

Historical Highlights

1736BC Revealed by archaeology as the earliest settlement date.

1643AD Abel Tasman sights the north-eastern islands of Taveuni.

1774 James Cook sights and lands at Vatoa Island in southern Lau.

1789 William Bligh sails through the islands in his ship's launch after the mutiny on HMS *Bounty* in Tonga.

1792 Bligh returns in the vessel, HMS *Providence*.

1799 American merchant ships *Ann* and *Hope* sail through Fiji.

1800 American schooner *Argo* is wrecked in Lau. Surviving crew bring a devastating epidemic, killing thousands of Fijians.

1804 Olive Slater discovers sandalwood in Vanua Levu and is responsible for the sandalwood trade until the logs are depleted in 1814.

1820 Marks the start of the *beche de mer* trade of cured sea slugs – dominated by American ships from Salem, New England.

1820–60 British and Yankee ships hunt sperm and humpback whales in Fijian waters.

1825 London Missionary Society attempts to establish mission but catechists remain in Tonga.

1835 Wesleyan Missionaries David Cargill and William Cross arrive from Tonga and settle at Lau.

1865 First attempt to form a Fiji confederacy as an experiment in a unified government fails

1867 The Tongan Chief Ma'afu forms the Northern Confederacy with some success.

1870 'Black birding', the kidnapping of people from other South Pacific Islands for cheap labour in Fiji, is brought to an end.

1871 Ratu Seru Cakobau declares himself the Tui Viti (King of Fiji) and forms a government at Levuka which survives for 3 years. Start of the Colo Wars.

1874 Fiji ceded to Britain. Measles epidemic claims 40,000 Fijians.

1877 Suva is the new capital.

1879 Indentured labour from India is introduced to provide labour on plantations.

1880 Development of sugar cane growing and processing industry.

1881 Rotuma becomes part of the Colony of Fiji.

1888 Birth of Ratu Sir Lala Sukuna, high chief, scholar and soldier of distinction.

1919 Indenture system ends officially. Most Indians decide to remain in the Fiji islands.

1928 Kingsford Smith arrives from Hawaii and lands at Albert Park on an epic transpacific flight.

1932 Gold discovered at Mt Kasi, Savusavu and Tavua in Viti Levu, where it is still mined today.

1939 World War II.

1942 Japanese occupy Banaba (Ocean Island); Fijians enlist and serve with distinction with the Allied forces in the Solomon Islands.

1952 Fijian troops leave for anti communist campaigns in Malaysia.

1958 Ratu Sir Lala Sukuna dies.

1970 Fiji becomes independent after 96 years of British rule.

1987 Two military coups against a coalition government comprising Fijians and Indians. Formation of an interim administration.

1992 General elections under new constitution guarantees ethnic Fijians majority of seats in parliament.

1997 A new constitution allowing a multi-racial government comes into effect.

1999 Elections return the Fiji Labour Party (FLP) in a landslide victory. Mahendra Pal Chaudry becomes prime minister.

2000 An attempted coup in May holds Chaudry and members of the FLP hostage in parliament for 56 six days by George Speight. The coup fails and an interim government is appointed under Laisenia Qarase.

2001 September elections sees Laisenia Qarase returned as head of an ethnic Fijian coalition government.

2005 Fiji prepares for the elections in 2006, wrestling with the knowledge that if a prime minister from the Indian community is elected, it may once again destabilise the government and cause political unrest.

South Pacific Ocean

Great Sea Reef

Cakaulevu

MACUATA-
I-WAI   Nadu

NADOGO   Navidamu   Natu

YAQAGA

YASAWA GROUP

Yasawairara

YASAWA

Navotua

NACULA

YADUA

Votua

Nasau

Bua   Navotuvotu
             842 m

Nabal

Dawara

Bligh Water

Nabouwalu

Soso

VIWA   NAVITI

WAYA

Namara

NAVADRA

KADOMO

NANANU-I-RA

MALAKE   NANANU-I-CAKE

Rakiraki

Barotu

Namarai

Tavua

Vatukoula

Nailaga   Ba

(Mt.Victoria)
Tomanivi
1323 m

Nadarivatu

Dawasamu

Wallevu

Nayavu

MAKOGAI

WAKAYA

Levuka

OVALAU

BATIKI

Vatu-i-ra Channel

YANUYA   TOKORIKI
MONU   TAVUA
MANA   TAI   Beachcomber
MALOLO   Resort

Lautoka

Natubua

Namaka

Bukuya

Nadrau

Laselevu

Korovou

Solevu

MALOLO
LAILAI

Nadi

Korolevu

Monasavo
1309 m

Toberua
Resort

Momi   Korovuto

Tuvu

Naraiyawa

Wainawaqa

Sawani

Nausori   Saw

Narewa

Namuamua

Nasirotu

Lokia

Lomawai   Semo

Suva

Sigatoka

Vatukarasa   Nabukelevu

Kalokolevu

Mau

Korolevu   Korovisilou

Galoa   Navua

VITI LEVU

BEQA   Dakuni

VATULELE

Kadavu Passage

Nabouwalu

ONO

Naikorokoro

Tavuki   Namara

Nasegai   Mokoisa   KADAVU

Fiji Islands

32 km / 20 miles

Day Itineraries

Fiji's 300 islands do not lend themselves to a quick and breezy visit. Many visitors are happy to be disposed by their travel agent to some island resort which offers dazzling white sand beaches beneath coconut palms and a lagoon of pastel greens, turquoises and deep blues. But for more intrepid explorers who want to pack in as much as possible within the space of their vacation, Fiji has much to offer. I have attempted to signpost in this book what I believe will not only be most enjoyable, but also the best value for money.

The main islands of Viti Levu and Vanua Levu comprise more than 80 percent of the total land mass. The International Airport is located at Nadi on the western side of Viti Levu, the largest island in the Fijian group. The airport also happens to be on the sunny 'dry' side of the island, within close proximity to the popular Yasawa and Mamanuca islands and the Coral Coast, a term used to describe the resort area from Momi Bay to the Pacific Harbour on Viti Levu.

Picture postcard beaches

The Nadi area on Viti Levu is where most of Fiji's resorts are found and the itineraries assume the visitor will spend at least the first few days here. But you could also choose to stay anywhere else on Viti Levu, or the surrounding islands for that matter, and still use the itineraries I've suggested.

The three day itineraries – a cruise to the Mamanuca Islands and two land tours on Viti Levu which span from the east to the southern coast and the westerly capital of Suva – are a wonderful introduction to Fiji as they take in the many diverse attractions of this island. Itinerary *Day 3* gives you the option of spending the night at Suva.

DAY 1

Day Cruise to Mamanuca Islands

There is no finer introduction to Fiji than a cruise from Nadi to the scattered island jewels of the nearby Mamanuca group. This is also a wonderful way to get over jet lag.

Several cruises leave each morning and return late in the afternoon. Buses pick guests up from hotels in the **Nadi** area and deliver them to the beach, ready for transfer to a cruise of their choice.

Prices vary according to the package offered, but lunch and a snorkelling tour or a coral-viewing cruise by glass-bottom boat are typically included. Day cruises cost between F$100 and F$120 per person, while overnight and longer trips are more expensive.

Captain Cook Cruises (tel: 6701823, www.captaincook.com.au) has a variety of cruise experiences, and these include a day cruise to the Mamanuca's pristine **Tivua Island**, lunch and dinner cruises, overnight trips by tall ship, and longer excursions by small ship.

Equally popular is **South Sea Cruises** (tel: 6750500, www.ssc.com.fj), which offers cruises via high-speed catamaran to a range of destinations, including the exclusive **Castaway Island** in the Mamanuca group, the relatively uninhabited **South Sea Island** just 25 minutes away from Nadi, and the remote **Yasawa Islands**. Semi-submersible reef-viewing cruises, as well as boat transfers to the various resorts in the Mamanuca Islands, are also available. Book directly or through your hotel tour desk.

For those who wish to strike out on their own, it is possible to hire a 'water taxi' for a day of island-hopping at your own pace. The price depends on the craft chosen, but can be as low as F$229 or as high as F$1,200 for the whole day. To protect Fiji's coral reefs, the government does not permit bareboat yacht charters, but visitors can rent both boat and skipper or a local guide for extended cruises through the islands. To do so, contact **Musket Cove Resort** (tel: 6662215, www.musketcovefiji.com) in the Mamanuca group, which has a range of yachts available for charter.

For those to pay considerably more than the going rate and enjoy the company of no more than 12 guests, I would recommend a cruise on *Whale's Tale*, a

A cruise on board the Whale's Tale

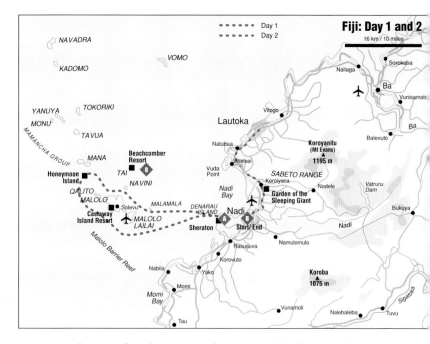

schooner-rigged motor yacht operated by **Oceanic Schooner Company** (tel: 6702443/6702444, e-mail: funcruises@connect. com.fj). This elegant schooner was created by American Paul Myers, who had sailed to Fiji on a lesser yacht in the mid-1970s. Myers was inspired by a dream. Ten years later, after several major events, including the death of the original shipbuilder, his boat was completed in Suva in 1984.

Sailing on the *Whale's Tale* is a sybaritic experience which begins the moment you board the beautiful 30-m (98-ft) luxury yacht and find a champagne breakfast awaiting your arrival. The breakfast, a sumptuous lunch and all beverages including beer, spirits and wines, as well as snorkelling gear are included in the price.

The anchor weighed, halyards pulled tight to set the sails, the adventure begins! *Whale's Tale* cruises past the islands of **Malamala**, **Navini**, **Malolo Lailai** and **Malolo** before reaching its own exclusive destination – **Honeymoon Island**. There is a magnificent beach here, with a colourful coral reef ideal for snorkelling.

The return voyage takes an alternative route around **Castaway Island** and the south-western side of Malolo and Malolo Lailai islands. *Whale's Tale* returns to its anchorage just before sunset, giving guests just enough time to enjoy the sunset and the torch-lighting ceremony on Denarau Island beach. The rate for adults is F$160, which is inclusive of pick-up from hotels in the Nadi area. Check with your hotel tour desk or travel agent for more information.

Aerial view of Malolo Lailai

DAY 2

Garden of the Sleeping Giant and Viseisei Village

A leisurely day starts in the foothills of the Sabeto mountain range, which includes a visit to the Garden of the Sleeping Giant and its profusion of orchids. Viseisei Village is next where you get a glimpse of Fijian village life. If time permits, visit the sugar producing town of Lautoka.

The **Garden of the Sleeping Giant** (open daily 9am–5pm; tel: 6722701; admission fee) occupies a lovely 20 hectares (50 acres) of gently sloping land at the base of the **Sabeto Range** and takes its name from the silhouette of a giant asleep on top of the mountains. It is a good place for spending a few hours, having a picnic among the orchids, lily ponds and forested walking tracks.

To get there, allow a 25-minute drive from the Nadi area towards Lautoka. Drive past the airport and when you have covered 5km (3 miles) you will arrive at the **Wailoko Road** turn-off. Look for a sign on a lamp post on the right-hand side and then turn right into Wailoko Road. Drive another 2km (1 mile) to the entrance of the garden – a verdant greenscape of bush, trees, ponds and more than 2,000 different types of orchids, some of which are native to Fiji.

For those who do not wish to drive, **United Touring Company Fiji** (open Mon–Sat 9am–5pm; tel: 6722811, e-mail: fiji@ utc.com.fj, www.atspacific.com/fiji, admission fee) can pick guests up from various hotels for a half-day tour to the Garden of the Sleeping Giant and Viseisei Village.

The garden has an interesting history. It was started by the late American actor Raymond Burr (from the television series *Perry Mason* and *Ironside*). At the time, Burr owned Naitauba Island in Lau, one of the prettiest in Fiji. When he decided to move, he sold it to a religious sect and transferred the orchid garden to a company in which he retained shares. Since then, the garden, destroyed by a number of hurricanes, has had to be replanted anew.

At the orchid garden, an attractive reception centre in the style of a Fijian *bure* (traditional thatched hut) has comfortable cane furniture for visitors to sit and admire the view and sip a cool fruit juice, before strolling through the gardens independently or joining an informative guided tour. A long walk through one shade house

A profusion of orchids

leads to a pond of water lilies, a bridge and a rest area and then continues through jungle interplanted with flowering trees and shrubs. There are seats where you can relax and absorb what you have seen.

Burr's former home in the hills, which overlooks **Saweni Bay** in the north of Nadi, still contains a few items that belonged to the superstar, including photographs, his favourite chair, and even his walking cane. The house is now owned by Don and Aileen Burness. Call them for information about touring the late actor's home (tel: 6662206; admission fee.)

Allow 10 minutes for your drive from the Garden of the Sleeping Giant to **Viseisei Village** (open daily 7am–6pm; donation) before continuing to Lautoka. Stories say that the ancestors of today's Fijians first arrived some 3,000 years ago at **Vuda Point** nearby ('vuda' means 'our ancestors'). The fact that the Chief of Viseisei, Ratu Josefa Iloilo, is the President of Fiji suggests the importance of the *matanitu* (state) in Fijian politics. In pre-European times, several parts of Fiji were recognised as *matanitu* – political confederations which owed allegiance to a paramount chief called a *tui*, the title incorporating the name of the area represented. Thus, the Tui Vuda is the head of the former 'state' of Vuda.

Viseisei Village was also once the home of the former late Prime Minister, Dr Timoci Bavadra, who was deposed in a military coup in 1987. An imposing *bure* was built for Dr Bavadra and is now very popular as a photographic subject. Take a left turn immediately after the bridge at the signpost. You will know you have arrived because of the road humps on the main highway.

Viseisei village has been open to the public for more than 20 years so there is no reason to feel you are intruding or disrupting the villagers' daily routine. **Viseisei** is a fairly wealthy: its residents own land on Vuda Point and on several offshore resort islands. Your gracious host at this village along Queen's Road is likely to be Mr Lusiana Kunaqoro (see www.fijianfamilies.com; e-mail: viseisei@fijianfamilies.com, or write to Box 7076, Lautoka, Fiji Islands). Your host will willingly offer to show visitors around the village, though it is mandatory to give a small gratuity to your guide before leaving. The merit of the visit is

The Tui Vuda (right) of Viseisei Village

Bird's eye view of Viseisei Village

not so much in seeing the village itself but for the opportunity of meeting the local people on their own turf and seeing something of their way of life.

It is now time to return to Nadi for lunch (see *Eating Out*, pages 70–74) and then an afternoon of shopping or relaxing on the beach. Alternatively, turn off to **Vuda Point Marina** (tel: 6668214) at the top of the hill for a light lunch or continue through a patchwork of sugar cane fields to **Lautoka**, sometimes called 'Sugar City', for a curry lunch at **Cyber Zone Netcafé** (159 Vitogo Parade, tel: 6651675), or Chinese food at the **Great Wall Of China** (52 Naviti St, tel: 6664763.) From the town of Lautoka, the gleaming jewels that make up the southern **Yasawa Islands** are clearly visible offshore.

From its humble beginnings as the base of the Colonial Sugar Refining Company, Lautoka has become Fiji's second largest city, after Suva, although it is small by international standards, with a population of only 30,000. Set against the beautiful Mt Evans (Koroyanitu) range, this waterfront town owes its existence primarily to a large sugar mill (said to be the biggest in the Southern Hemisphere) and a deep water port. Although there is not a lot by way of tourist interest here, the city is economically important to Fiji. Lautoka is not only the base of the sugar industry (now in transition), it has also acquired new status as the site of a new tax-free industrial zone. Check out the large produce and handicraft marketplace near the bus station, where buses leave for Suva via Kings Road to the north, and via Queens Road to the south. You may also wish to visit the new **Hare Krishna Temple** (5 Tavewa Ave, tel: 6641112; donation) and the **Fijian Sugar Company Compound** district, with its old colonial homes and 100-year-old banyan trees. A sugar cane railway runs through the centre of the town between a line of tall royal palm trees.

DAY ③

Nadi to Suva

Travel to the charming capital city of Suva via Queen's Road; driving past scenic sugar cane fields, forests of lush Caribbean pine trees and isolated bays. Then, cut across the township of Sigatoka to a Tongan Fort, the resorts on the Coral Coast, Kula Eco Park, and finally to Pacific Harbour.

It is about 197km (122 miles) from Nadi to the capital city, Suva. This journey will require up to 3 hours of driving with stops for photography on the way. This will time your arrival in Suva for lunch. If you wish to avoid the long drive back, plan to have more stops along the way, arrive in the early evening and spend the night at Suva.

Coral Coast spans from Nadi to Su

The alternative, if you do not wish to drive yourself, is to book a guided tour of Suva with **United Touring Company Fiji** (tel: 6722811, e-mail: fiji@utc.com.fj, www.atspacific.com/fiji).

Because of the distance you will be covering and the spectacular

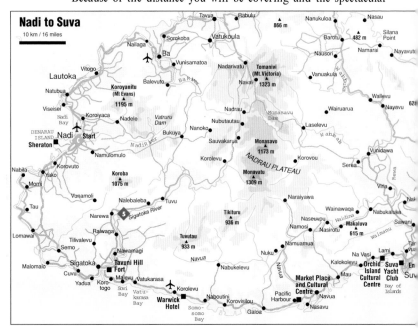

scenery along the way, a self-drive day trip to Suva should begin early in the morning. An 8am start is ideal. The road is well maintained and tarred all the way. The only hazards are incompetent drivers who overtake at blind corners, or who stop abruptly on the road without pulling to the side; and horses and cattle, which, unrestrained by fences, wander where they please. Allow an hour or so to reach the town of Sigatoka.

Sigatoka is a pleasant little town on the banks of Fiji's second largest river and benefits from both the farming community and the tourist resorts along the Coral Coast. The site of a former Tongan chief's fortification on the southern side of the river, **Tavuni Hill Fort** (tel: 6520818; open Mon–Sat 8am–5pm; admission fee), is one of the most interesting sights in the area. Forts such as this are found all over Fiji, but the Tavuni Hill Fort is among the most accessible for visitors.

Here guides, said to be descendants of the Tongans, will show visitors the head-chopping stones where cannibalistic sacrifices used to be performed, as well as a ceremonial ground and a couple of grave sites. A 90-m (295-ft) steep ridge at the edge of a bend in the Sigatoka River, an obvious strategic location for a defence site, offers

View of the Korotogo resorts

panoramic views of the coastline and the rich Sigatoka river valley. To reach the fort, cross the bridge and take the first left turn which will bring you back to the river and the old bridge. Turn right at the old bridge and follow the river upstream. It is 4km (2½ miles) from the turn-off. Also within convenient access from here is the Sigatoka Sand Dunes National Park (see *itinerary* on page 33).

About 7km (4¼ miles) past the bridge is the village of **Korotogo**, which is located where the highway joins the **Coral Coast**. From here, the next 35km (21¾ miles) runs beside the lagoon and through a series of villages and resorts. Korotogo marks the southern boundary of the sugar cane growing area. The landscape begins to change as you head towards the south-east. As the prevailing trade winds carry moisture and dump it on this coast, the vegetation is lush and the rainforest stretches over hills and mountains. There are six resorts in the Korotogo area, including the five-star **Outrigger On the Lagoon**, a luxury resort hotel, and other small, more intimate hotels which offer accommodation and cater for every budget and taste.

Bird's eye view of Outrigger on the Lagoon

Opposite, northeast of the Outrigger hotel, is **Kula Eco Park** (tel: 6500505, open daily 10am–4pm; www.fijiwild.com; admission fee), formerly a bird park, now redeveloped as a wildlife sanctuary and educational centre for children. Nestling in a valley of coastal forest less than 1km (½ mile) from the Pacific Ocean, the park is dedicated to the conservation of Fiji's wildlife. Its primary objective is to provide a captive breeding programme for endangered animal species, in particular, Fiji's crested and banded iguanas as well as the endangered peregrine falcon.

The next village you will come to is **Malevu**. The road skirts around **Bulu Bay** and then skirts the more open **Sovi Bay**. The southern side of Sovi Bay is popular with locals. It offers safe swimming away from the crashing surf which at times sweeps into the bay. This is a good spot for a swim break – there are parking places by the side of the road – and a picnic lunch.

Next is the village of **Vatukarasa**. It is laid out in the old Fijian pattern with a handsome chief's *bure* next to the road as you first enter the village, a wide village green with houses and *bure*s on each side and a church at the far end. The opening into Vatukarasa Bay is wide and at times allows a big swell to roll in and crash onto the beach. You will pass the resorts of **Tabua Sands**, the **Hideaway** and **Naviti**, each tucked away among flowers and coconut trees next to its own beach and then reach **Korolevu**, the former site of Fiji's first beach resort. The original resort closed some years ago but the new **Naviti Resort**, cocooned in 15 hectares (38 acres) of lush gardens and fringed with golden sand beaches, is an elegant replacement. At the other end of the bay

Fiji's Collared Lory

is the **Warwick of Fiji**, which was formerly the Hyatt Regency.

The stretch of road between **Korotogo** and **Naboutini** is particularly attractive. It winds around bays and climbs low ridges for views of villages and lagoons glimpsed through av-

Canoeists at the Outrigger

enues of coconut palms and rainforest, then moves away from the coast, climbs a series of low hills and emerges on the coast to briefly join the sea again before reaching the wide expanse of open flat land at **Pacific Harbour**. The islands of **Yanuca** and **Beqa** are visible offshore.

Planned as an upmarket housing and tourism development, Pacific Harbour was one of Fiji's most ambitious projects. Hundred of acres of lowland were cleared and drained; lakes were created; and an 18-hole championship golf course designed by Robert Trent Jones Jr and a grand clubhouse were built. New hotels were constructed beside the beach and the whole area was dubbed 'The Adventure Capital of Fiji', as it offers a diverse array of activities, including scuba diving, surfing and river rafting. The area is also good for shopping and watching sunsets. In addition, Beqa Lagoon offshore has world-class diving sites and a surf break (see *itinerary* on page 42).

The **Market Place and Cultural Centre** (open daily 7.30am–6.30pm) built around a waterway, is an ideal place for another break. There is an assortment of curio shops and restaurants, and regular tours are conducted on the waterway. Here is the place to catch one of the periodic firewalking demonstrations.

From Pacific Harbour, the road runs through a wide plain. The township of **Navua** is on the eastern bank of the river where land is held in small holdings by Indian farmers who specialise in rice cultivation (see *Navua River Trip* itinerary on page 41).

About 4km (2½ miles) before you reach centre of Suva is the **Bay of Islands** and the attractive suburb of **Lami**. The **Tradewinds Hotel** sits on the water's edge; yachts and pleasure craft are moored in the bay in the lee of three islands, and there is a convention centre beside the lagoon. From here, it is 3km (1¾ miles) to the heart of the city, passing through the **Walu Bay** industrial area and the **Royal Suva Yacht Club**.

You can either opt to spend the night at **Suva** and tour the colourful town the following morning (see *Pick & Mix*, page 30), or, if you arrive early enough, tour Suva and then drive back to Nadi on the same day. The **Holiday Inn** (tel: 3301600) along Victoria Parade is a comfortable walk from the city centre. For dinner, the **O'Reilley's** (tel: 3312968) complex is always popular as are the **Golden Dragon** and **Traps** bars along Victoria Parade.

PICK & MIX

A half-day tour of the capital city of Suva. Take in the city sights and revel in this melting pot of a dozen different races.

Begin your walking tour at the **Thurston Gardens** (open daily 8am–5pm, free), on the grounds in which the **Fiji Museum** (Mon–Thur 8am–4.30pm, Fri 8am–4pm, Sat 9am–4pm; admission fee) is found. Established in 1904, the museum holds comprehensive collection of Fijian artefacts as well as a collection from other Pacific islands. A double-hulled canoe built in 1900 commands the main hall. The somewhat unkempt Thurston Gardens houses an interesting collection of South Pacific flora.

Return to **Victoria Parade** and turn left to Queen Elizabeth Drive. This brings you to the gates of **Government House**, the state residence of the President of Fiji. A guard dressed in a red tunic and white *sulu* (sarong) at the gate is a favourite photographic

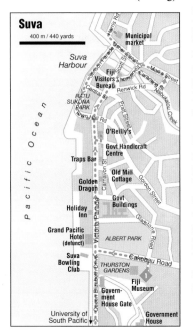

subject. If you continue beside the sea, you will reach the **University of the South Pacific** campus, built on a former seaplane base. The base played a critical role in the war in the Pacific against invading Japanese by mounting long-range reconnaissance missions and mercy flights saving many lives.

Retrace your steps up Queen Elizabeth Drive to the main drag of Victoria Parade, past Albert Park on your right and the Holiday Inn on your left. Turn right into Macarthur Street opposite O'Reilly's and allow 2 hours to explore the heart of the city's commercial section. The **Government Handicraft Centre** (tel: 3315899; Mon–Fri 7am–6pm, Sat 8am–5pm) sells a wide range of Fijian handicrafts, including replicas of old weapons, bowls, basketware, and *masi* (bark) cloth items, and is well worth a visit, though prices can sometimes a bit high. Beware of pickpockets.

Retrace your steps to Victoria Parade, turn right and continue north. Cross Townhall Road to **Ratu Sukuna Park** on the left. Here, Renwick Road joins Victoria Parade at the triangle with an old *ivi* (native chestnut) tree at its apex. Much of old Suva still survives along **Renwick Road**. Victoria Parade joins Thomson Street crosses Nabukalou Creek and turns into Cumming Street which in turn joins Renwick Road. Look out for Fijian women selling handicrafts under the flamboyant tree on the corner of Thomson and Cumming streets. Duty-free dealers also crowd each other here, the oldest unchanged part of Suva.

Stroll up Cumming Street, turn left into Renwick Road, and then left again to Marks Street, which will take you to the Thomson Street junction. Continue towards Usher Street to the **Municipal Market** (open daily 7am–5pm), taking extra care to avoid 'sword sellers' (see *Shopping*, page 69) and 'guides' who will offer to take you to places where you will get the 'best deal'.

The Municipal Market offers a fascinating glimpse of Fiji's multiracial community. All the products of land, lagoon and ocean are on display here. From the markets, follow **Stinson Parade** along the foreshore, past Ratu Sukuna Park and eventually back to Victoria Parade. Have lunch at one of the restaurants at **O'Reilley's** (tel: 3312968), just before the Macarthur Street turning, or at the **Old Mill Cottage Café Restaurant** (tel: 3312134) at Carnavon Street.

From here, you might wish to visit the **Colo-i-Suva Forest Park** (Forestry Station tel: 3320211; admission fee). Occupying some 245 hectares (605 acres) of forest in the hills north of Suva, about 11km (7 miles) away from the capital, the place has natural swimming pools and walking trails, and is also a bird-watcher's haven. To get there, take the Sawani bus from the Suva City bus station, or drive along Princes Road out of Suva, past Tamavua and Tacirua villages.

Clock tower, Thurston Gardens

2. Natadola Beach Picnic and Coral Coast Railway

See the historic Momi Bay guns; picnic at Natadola Beach, popular with the locals on weekends; ride the toy train Coral Coast Railway; and visit the spectacular Sigatoka Sand Dunes.

Pack a hearty picnic lunch for the day and drive out on the **Queen's Highway** towards Suva. The first point of interest is found 15km (9¼ miles) away from town at the Momi Bay turn-off – the **Momi Bay Battery Historical Park** (tel: 3301807; free). The two guns here – one named Queen Victoria (1900) and the other Edward VIII (1901) – were set up in 1941 by the New Zealand army to defend the southern approach to Nandi Bay. They are World War II relics and have been restored by the National Trust of Fiji.

Follow the signposts to the location. The guns and the grounds which overlook **Momi Bay** and the main channel in the barrier reef are not spectacular, but may be of interest to those fascinated by the Pacific phase of World War II.

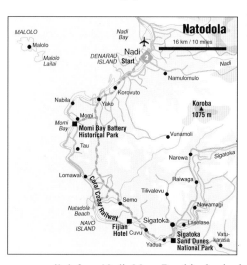

The **Mamanuca Islands** are clearly visible from here and, in fact, this is the closest point to the islands. Return again to the main road and continue south towards Suva.

It takes about 25 minutes to reach the Natadola Beach turn-off at **Maro Road**, some 40km (25 miles) from Nadi. Maro Road is clearly signposted and the turn-off is easy to find. This is still the heart of the sugar cane country and the road twists and winds its way to the sea between sugar cane farms and mosques. Cross the river twice and this will confirm that you are on the right road. Keep bearing left. Allow 15 minutes for a comfortable drive from the turn-off before arriving at **Natadola Beach**.

There is more than a mile of magnificent white sand curving in a pastel arc from Navo island in the south to the north west. As the prevailing trade wind blows in from the land, the extensive bay is usually calm: ideal conditions for windsurfing. Coral reefs encompass the bay to nearly a mile offshore where a wide passage allows safe entry into the bay. Yachtsmen tend to avoid this anchorage because the wide entrance allows a swell from the south to roll into the bay causing boats to rock uncomfortably. But the same swell will sometimes produce a low surf ideal for body surfing. The beach is popular with locals who congregate here on weekends picnicking or enjoying barbecues.

Picturesque Natadola Beach

The only hotel here is the **Natadola Beach Resort** (tel: 6511251, www.natadola.com), which features 11 guest rooms and has a restaurant and bar, both of which are open to the public. It also provides public changing rooms for day visitors arriving on guided tours. Coral reefs on each side of the bay offer good snorkelling, while horses-for-hire offer a good alternative to swimming.

Continue on the main highway for another 15 minutes to the **Coral Coast Railway** (open daily, tel: 6520434) terminal at the **Shangri-la Fijian Resort & Spa** turn-off. Located just outside the hotel, the railway uses two restored sugar cane trains for tours on narrow-gauge railroads through the cane fields, across bridges and along the coast. The most popular tour runs 14-km (9-mile) north to Natadola Beach, departing in the morning and taking visitors back in the late afternoon. The other locomotive travels east to Sigatoka on the Coral Coast, while a half-day version of this trip takes visitors to Sigatoka town for shopping and sightseeing. The railway is part of the network that was established by the Colonial Sugar Refining Company when it developed the sugar industry. The trains once hauled raw sugar cane to Lautoka for processing.

If time permits, continue another 10km (6¼ miles) by road to the **Sigatoka Sand Dunes National Park** (visitor centre tel: 6520343, admission fee), one of the most arresting sights in Fiji. Designated Fiji's first National Park in 1989, the sand dunes cover 650 hectares (1,600 acres) of coastline. A resource centre just off the main road on the right has a vivid graphic display and a walkway which allows visitors to ascend the dunes for panoramic views. Follow this road to the dunes,

All aboard!

park your car and ascend the dunes for panoramic views of the sea, the **Sigatoka River** where it meets the ocean, and the dunes. The highest point of the sand dunes rises no more than 30½m (100ft) above sea level, but they are spectacular nevertheless.

Some of Fiji's most important archaeological finds were made on these sands. The winds constantly expose pottery shards and sometimes human remains. The oldest human remains to have been found in the Fiji-Polynesian part of the Pacific came from this site. Fresh water from the Sigatoka River has impaired coral growth and as there is no barrier reef, a large surf usually thunders onto the exposed beach. The beach here is the haunt of surfers and wind-surfers, but only strong swimmers and experienced surfers should venture into the sea here.

3. Nausori Highlands

Hire a four-wheel drive, prepare a picnic lunch, pack swimming gear and set off to explore something of Fiji's wilderness. Make an early start for a full day of adventure. There are two different routes to choose from, both with equally breathtaking and rugged scenery. Do not attempt both itineraries on the same day.

This is a tour for the experienced driver as the roads can be very treacherous. The car rental company will insist on an indemnity clause for your four-wheel drive vehicle as some cars have been damaged through careless or incompetent driving.

Route 1: Allow 15 minutes from Nadi to the Nausori Highlands road turn-off. The easiest way is to drive south (towards Suva) through the town and turn left at the service station. There is a Hindu temple on the opposite side of the road. Follow this road for 5km (3 miles) and keep your eyes peeled for the **Nausori Highlands** signpost on your right.

From there, it's 34-km (21-miles) to the Bukuya turn-off. The road leaves the Nadi flats and begins ascending over rolling country of sugar cane farms towards the highlands. It then turns steeply uphill and follows a narrow ridge with sharp bends.

A 4-wheel drive is a must

Massive volcanic rocks and sheer cliff faces overlooking Nadi town, the airport and the offshore islands offer good subjects for photography.

There is a forestry station and village at **Nausori** when you reach the top. Once the site of a sawmill, this is now the centre of an ambitious replanting programme with Caribbean pine. The road leaves the plantations and continues through the rainforest. On the right is the **Sigatoka River** catch-

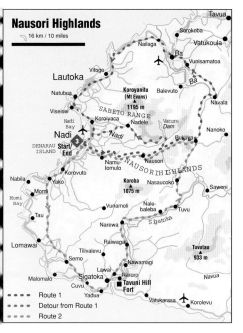

Nausori Highlands

16 km / 10 miles

Tavua
Sorokoba
Vatukoula
Nailaga
Ba
Vunisamatoa
Vitogo
Lautoka
Koroyanitu (Mt Evans) 1195 m
Balevuto
Natubua
Navala
SABETO RANGE
Viseisei
Koroiyaca
Nadi Bay
Nadele
Vaturu Dam
Nanoko
Nadi
Bukuya
DENARAU ISLAND
Start/End
Namu-Iomulo
Nausori
NAUSORI HIGHLANDS
Korovuto
Nabila
Koroba 1075 m
Nasaucoko
Saweni
Yako
Momi
Momi Bay
Vunamoli
Nale-baleba
Tuvu
Tau
Narewa
Sigatoka
Lomawai
Raiwaqa
Tilivalevu
Tuvutau 933 m
Semo
Nawamagi
Lawai
Naroro
Navua
Malomalo
Sigatoka
Cuvu
Tavuni Hill Fort
Yadua
Vatukarasa
Korolevu

- - - - Route 1
- - - - Detour from Route 1
- - - - Route 2

ment while to the left is the **Nadi River**. A turn-off on the left marks the access to **Vaturu Dam** – the source of fresh water for Nadi and Lautoka.

For those who want a less adventurous trip, turn left to the dam and after a picnic lunch, descend via the **Sabeto Valley** to the main highway north of the airport. Otherwise, continue on towards **Bukuya** for another 12km (7½ miles) and turn left before reaching the village. The road now follows the **Ba River** catchment towards the village of picture-perfect **Navala**, 17km (10½ miles) from the junction. On the way there are plenty of picturesque spots to stop for a picnic.

Some time ago, the chief and people of Navala made the decision to keep the village traditional and allow only *bures* to be built for housing. As a result, Navala is a remarkable village and an ideal subject for photography. The village also accepts visitors who wish to stay the night. Sunday is 'family day' and therefore not a good time. The usual Fijian courtesies should be followed if you intend to visit. This requires paying for the presentation of 1kg (2lb) of *yaqona* (the mildy narcotic powdered root of the piper mysthisticum plant) to the *turaga ni koro* (village headman) with the request that

Road between Bukuya and Navala Village

Down the Ba River in a bilibili

you wish to look around the village and take some photographs. Details are available on www.fijianfamilies.com.

Allow an hour's careful driving from Navala, 18km (11¼ miles) away, to reach the township of **Ba**. As you descend from Navala, the road passes the sugar cane farms and the compounds of Indian farmers and their families. Some of the fields are perched on ledges, offering testimony to the ingenuity of the farmers. On leaving Navala, the **Ba River** enters a gorge, the site of Fiji's whitewater rafting. The excitement of the ride depends on the volume of water in the river and, for this reason, rafting is best after a heavy downpour in the highlands.

The road begins its descent to Ba from a high ridge overlooking the lowlands and the sparkling sea in the distance. Much like the road up to the Nausori Highlands, it is steep and winding until it reaches low ground. The road is tarred some miles before the township and passes by the sugar mill on the banks of the river. The town itself is a quaint one-street collection of shops. Bear ahead at the roundabout, keeping the service station on your left, until you reach the T-junction and turn left to cross the Ba River by the new bridge. You will know you are on the right road when you cross a one-way bridge where traffic is regulated by traffic lights which no one seems to take much notice of. The western side of the river has some rather ostentatious houses built by prosperous Indian merchants. It is now 72km (44¾ miles) from Ba to Nadi and 38km (23½ miles) to Lautoka on a tarred highway. Allow 1¼ hours and an extra 15 minutes during the sugar cane harvest season when you may encounter slow-moving trucks carting cane to the mill. The section between Ba and Lautoka offers great views of sugar cane fields and pine tree plantations on steep hills, and in the distance, Bligh Water and the Yasawa Islands.

The distances involved are not great but because of the road condition, this route, with a stop for a swim and picnic and then a visit to Navala village, will require a whole day.

Route 2: An alternative route, but just as spectacular, is to drive from Nadi onto the Queen's Highway to Sigatoka town, 77km (48 miles) away, and from there up the Sigatoka Valley road. This will eventually bring you back to Nadi through the Nausori Highlands.

There are many points of interest along this route. The site of a a Tongan hill fort (see page 27) at Naroro seen on the opposite side of the river is worth a visit. Cross the river and turn left and then right at the old bridge to Kavanagasau. From here, it is 4km (2½ miles) to the village. From its vantage point, the old fort once commanded the

Sigatoka River and still offers breathtaking views. Return to the Nadi side of the river and turn right up the valley road to the village of **Lawai** where pottery is still made in the time-honoured Fijian way.

The bountiful fertility of the **Sigatoka River Valley** has earned it the title of the 'salad bowl' of Fiji. A full range of vegetables thrive in the rich soils here, and a government agricultural research station, 6½km (4 miles) from town, is constantly experimenting with new varieties and species. The road up the valley is not tarred and requires attentive driving. It follows the river for most of the way and climbs two steep ridges, offering magnificent scenery. There are villages on the way and 35km (21¾ miles) up the road, tobacco-drying kilns are a distinct landmark at **Nalebaleba**. About 7km (4¼ miles) further, a road on the left leads to Bukuya while the valley road continues to its terminal at Korolevu. Follow the road to Bukuya. There are two villages, both with access roads on the way. The first is **Nasaucoko** village, headquarters of government troops during the Colo War against the mountain people in 1876, two years after the cession of Fiji to Britain. It was here that some of the rebel leaders were hanged and the war brought to an end.

It is 17km (10½ miles) from the time you leave the valley road and reach the village of **Bukuya**. A little way past the village, take the turn to the left which will eventually leads you back to Nadi. Allow at least 5 hours for each of the two excursions, plus extra time for swimming, picnicking and photography. Alternatively, check with your hotel tour desk for a number of interesting highlands tour options, including a fascinating excursion to a former fortress in a massive cave. This tour, known as the

Navala village, Viti Levu

Cave Tour (see page 40), also offers lunch, a *yaqona* ceremony at the village and a ride on a *bilibili*, a local bamboo raft. The Naihehe Caves were last used as a fortress and refuge during the Colo War when mountain tribes rebelled against the colonial government.

4. Levuka: Fiji's Old Capital

There is no question that the town of Levuka, on the island of Ovalau, off the eastern coast of Viti Levu is a special place. Time seems to stand still here and those who venture beyond the usual tourist traps will be delightfully surprised with their discovery. This day trip will take in all the major attractions of Levuka.

Levuka town, the former Fijian capital, sits on a narrow strip of land with a bush-clad mountain directly at its back. The town was important for three reasons: the direction of the prevailing east-south-east trade winds which allowed sailing ships to enter and leave port without difficulty; its central position on the south-west coast of the island of Ovalau within the Lomaiviti group of islands; and finally, its proximity to the once politically powerful states of Bau, Verata, Rewa and Cakaudrove. When Fiji became a British possession in 1874, Levuka's days as the capital were numbered.

Colourful characters associated with the town include the swash-

Beach Street in sleepy Levuka

buckling buccaneer Billy Hayes, poet Rudyard Kipling, writer Somerset Maughan, and WWI German naval raider Count von Luckner. Levuka is also a town of many Fijian 'firsts': first bank, post office, school, newspaper, masonic lodge, private members' club, municipality, hospital, town hall and public electric system. The Royal Hotel, at over 140 years, is the oldest operating hotel in the South Pacific. The sleepy little frontier town of 2,000 inhabitants retains many of its pre- and post-colonial buildings and is considered the most intact remaining example of colonial influence in the South Pacific.

The fact that Levuka did not decline completely after the capital was moved to Suva is due to a fish cannery operated by the Pacific Fishing Company, which buys skip-jack tuna from local and overseas contract fishermen and indirectly pumps money into the local economy. The cannery is located next to the wharf at the southern end of **Beach Street**, the town's main (and only) thoroughfare. A stroll around the town will take no more than 20 minutes. This will allow a thorough look at most of the town's historic landmarks: the **Catholic Church**, with the cross on the bell tower that also serves as one of the lead-in lights into the harbour; **Levuka**

Levuka town on the island of Ovalau

Public School, which is the oldest in the country; the **Ovalau Club**; the old **Town Hall** just beside the club; the **Masonic Lodge**; the **Royal Hotel**; and the **Totoga Falls**, reached by following a track from the end of Bath Road. For some excellent views, walk the 199 steps up **Mission Hill**.

Approximately 1km (½ mile) south of the cannery is **Nasova** and its commemorative park. This is where Fiji was ceded to Britain in 1874 and where in 1970, Prince Charles on behalf of his mother, Queen Elizabeth II, returned Fiji to the descendants of the chiefs who had given it to Queen Victoria 96 years ago.

The more adventurous should linger a day or so. Other than the old Royal Hotel (tel: 3440024, www.royallevuka.com), visitors can stay at **Levuka Homestay** (tel: 3440777, www.levukahomestay.com), or **Ovalau Holiday Resort** (tel: 3440329). Offshore full-facility resorts include the super-luxurious **Wakaya Club** (tel: 3448128, www.wakaya.com) as well as the more modest **Naigani Island Resort** (tel: 3312069) and the **Leleuvia Island Backpackers' Resort** (tel: 3301584).

Both the **Levuka Community Centre** (Mon–Fri 9am–5pm, Sat 9am–noon; admission fee) and **Ovalau Watersports** (tel: 3440166; www.owlfiji.com) organise hiking trips to inland villages, island tours and other activities.

The quickest way of getting to Levuka is by **Air Fiji** (tel: 3313666, www.airfiji.com.fj), which offers two flights daily (Mon–Sat) and one flight on Sunday. For those with more time to spare, the **Patterson Brothers Shipping Company** (tel: 3315644) operates a 5-hour daily ferry between Suva and Levuka. For visitors who arrive on Ovalau Island by plane from the mainland, there is a bumpy bus service between the airport and the township. Once in Levuka, taxis and 'carriers' are available to take visitors to any part of the island.

The fascinating Naihehe Caves in the upper Sigatoka River Valley are found in a mountain of marble more than 48km (30 miles) from the sea even though at one time they were formed in the sea. The huge caves were also an impregnable fortress in Fiji's recent blood-thirsty past.

Tours to the **Naihehe Caves** are organised by **Adventures in Paradise** (tel: 6520833, e-mail: wfall@connect.com.fj; www.adventuresinparadisefiji.com). Enquire at your hotel tour desk or book your trip with the tour company directly. The tour includes a knowledgeable guide, who will explain the history of the valley, especially its relation to a settlement of Tongan warriors. There is

Blowing the sacred conch a traditional *yaqona* welcome ceremony at the village, a tour of the caves, a ride downriver on a *bilibili* bamboo raft and a picnic lunch at the village.

The caves were last used as a refuge and fortress to the last rebel cannibal tribes in Fiji in the 1875–76 Colo Wars when mountain tribesmen swept down the valley to attack and cannibalise Christians on the coast. Troops dispatched by the governor eventually quelled the rebellion but not before the people of Toga village had sought refuge in their fortress cave.

Today, the family of the *Na Bete* (heathen priest) are the guardians and guides of the caves. The approach is via a walkway through a forest. A stream marks the entrance to the cave and requires you to stoop low under an overhang to get in. Once you enter, the cave opens into a series of huge chambers. The chambers have specific uses with the best parts reserved for the chief and the *Na Bete*. There are areas for sleeping, a maternity ward and a special area where human sacrifices were performed and the flesh cooked.

The bilibili raft and children of Toga village

When the cave tour is completed it's time to go down to the river where bamboo rafts wait to take you downstream. The raft voyage ends near the village where a picnic lunch awaits, followed by the return trip by road. Be sure to take plenty of film as the ride up the river offers many photographic opportunities.

6. Navua River Trip

A river journey up the Navua River, followed by a traditional welcome and lunch at Namuamua Village.

The best way to enjoy this tour is to book with **United Touring Company** (tel: 6722811; e-mail: fiji@utc.com.fj) either directly or through your hotel tour desk. The bus picks guests up from the Nadi hotels from 8am and along the Coral Coast resorts and it arrives at **Navua** township on the banks of the **Navua River** at about 11.30am. A tour guide offers useful commentary along the way.

As Navua town is only 20 minutes from Suva, the trip covers most of the **Queen's Highway** and offers spectacular vistas of sugar cane fields and pine tree forests, with coastal views that delight with the ever-changing colours of the lagoon glimpsed through tall coconut trees.

But the drive, pleasant as it is, is only an appetiser for the main course – the boat ride up the Navua River to Na-

Navua River Trip
16 km / 10 miles

muamua village. Navua town itself, which serves the farmers of the river delta, is small and rather slow. Many of the quaint buildings are reminiscent of an earlier vintage. A market-place spills over onto the footpath and the edge of the road.

Among the many flat-bottom, narrow punts at the jetty are some that bring produce to the market every morning and return upriver later in the day. One of these takes visitors to Namuamua village.

Seated two abreast, hip to hip, the boat has only a few inches of freeboard. The pilot cranks the outboard engine, the guide sits forward and the voyage begins. About 40 minutes after leaving Navua, the punt passes the village of **Nakavu**, the last village with a road access. The river then enters a gorge flanked by bush-clad hills, tall tree ferns, vine-clad tree trunks, clumps of bright green, fluffy

Punting up the Navua River

bamboo and small grassy banks. The river narrows and the punt, like a homing salmon, finds the line of least resistance up frothing rapids. Keep your eyes peeled for spectacular waterfalls as they tumble down cliff faces, some flashing like silver behind a screen of bamboo, others majestic as they gush 30m (98ft) into the river. It takes another 40 minutes to reach the Namuamua village. If the water level is low, the punt requires manhandling over the shallows, a function performed by the boatmen while you sit tight.

As the punt emerges from the gorge, the country opens up gradually. **Nukusere** village, high on the bank, is the first major settlement. A few hundred metres ahead, on the opposite bank, is the village of **Namuamua**.

School children awaiting your arrival at the riverbank lead you up into a house where a presentation of *yaqona* is made on your behalf. Once the *yaqona is* served, the guide takes the group on a tour of the village.

After a hearty lunch eaten from pandanus mats covering the floor, there is a *meke* or communal dance put up by a group of young men. The formal entertainment complete, the band invite you to dance. Leave the village at 3pm, and you will arrive at Navua town by 4pm; the trip downriver takes much less time.

Navua town is also the port of departure for the volcanic island of **Beqa**, located about 16km (10 miles) offshore. Beqa is the home of the legendary firewalkers who are from the island – more specifically, from Rukua. The island is great for hiking, and its barrier reef also features several beautiful islets within its lagoon, and is recognised as one of the world's top 10 dive sites. The reef also has a number of passages, including **Frigate Passage**, which is popular with surfers and well

A drink of yaqona… followed by lunch

known for its magnificent left-hand waves.

Accommodation on Beqa comes in the form of two resorts – **Beqa Lagoon Resort** (tel: 3450100, www.lagoonresort.com), where barefoot staff welcome you onshore to one of 25 *bures*, and the luxurious **Lalati Resort** (tel: 3472033, www.lalati-fiji.com). Both offer snorkelling and scuba diving facilities.

Right: a waterfall seen on the way up Navua River

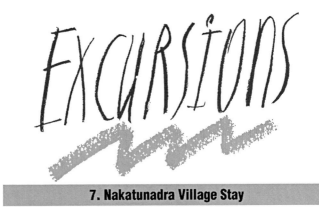

EXCURSIONS

7. Nakatunadra Village Stay

A few days' stay at a Fijian village will provide an interesting insight into traditional life, and a chance to experience Fijian hospitality and warmth at its best. For more information about staying in Fijian villages, visit www.fijianfamilies.com.

Village stays allow visitors the opportunity of experiencing the full gamut of Fijian experience, from shrimp catching and spear fishing to wild pig hunting. To allow the village you would like to visit to prepare for your arrival, the **Fijian Families Network** (www.fijianfamilies.com) requires that reservations be made in advance.

One such village you might visit is the **Nakatunadra village** (nakatunadra@fijianfamilies.com), located near Rakiraki, north of Viti Levu. It features traditional *bures*, gracious people, a nearby thermal spring and a traditional fort.

A 2-hour drive on King's Road from Nadi airport will take you to the village, where the heads of five families await your visit. Your host is likely to be **Apisalome Ragolea**.

In making your arrangements, the following should be the rule: Allow about F$40 for each guest per night for accommodation and food. Additional items such as cans of corned beef, rice, sugar, tea and flour – regarded as luxuries by the villagers – should be purchased in Nadi for sharing with your host family. The quantity you need to buy depends on the intended length of stay. An additional F$5 should be allowed for a guide for each day that one is

Preparing yaqona for the welcome ceremony

Villagers and their guests

required. The guide will be a villager who will be happy to show you around, take you hiking, and perhaps also hunting for wild boar or fishing in the river. Do take a casting rod with you if you enjoy fishing.

Many village activities can be experienced without prior planning. The women can go fishing for prawns and fish, while the men can go to plantations or hunt for wild boar. In the late afternoon there may be a game of touch rugby or volleyball, followed by a bath in the river and a bowl of *yaqona*. In the evening, villagers and guests may gather to tell stories, play the guitar and sing, and dance. You may ask many questions. Fijians will happily answer any polite question you ask them, and they will also expect the same of you.

Fijian etiquette requires the presentation of *yaqona* – the mildly narcotic root of the *Piper methysticum* plant – to your hosts and the whole village will assemble to accept the offering. One half kilo (1lb) of *yaqona* is more than ample and will cost between F$30 and F$40, depending on the market rate. Local people often cultivate *yaqona* so it is best to purchase it at the village and contribute cash to the village economy.

There are a few other rules of etiquette to observe during a village stay. Remove your footwear when entering a house or any *pandanus*-mat covered areas. Dress modestly – no short shorts, bathing suits or bare shoulders – and do not wear a hat, as that's considered very rude. Never touch a Fijian on the head or tousle their hair, as it is considered the ultimate insult. It is likely all adults in your group will be invited to a *yaqona* (or grog) session. You may be asked to buy a piece of *yaqona* root to present to the group leader (about F$8 to $10). If this does not happen, leave a donation for receiving the *yaqona*. Quietly sit cross-legged on the floor as the brew is prepared. Do not step on or over the small cord extending snakelike along the floor from the *tanoa* (wooden *yaqona* bowl); this is considered the Fijian link to the spirit world. Down a coconut-shell cupful in one gulp; then, with your palms held in a cupped position, softly clap your hands twice and say 'thank you'. *Yaqona* is mildly hypnotic or merely lip numbing and is claimed to alleviate stress without impairing alertness. It is also reputed to relieve headaches, muscle aches and improve hearing along with a wide range of other benefits. Try it for yourself and see.

Women dancers

No stay in Fiji is quite complete without a stay at one of its many island resorts, each of which has its own personality. Beachcomber Resort in the Mamanuca island group caters for varied tastes.

The great Viti Levu barrier reef sweeps in an arc to the north from Momi to the Yasawa Islands and then continues to the north-western extremity of Vanua Levu at Udu Point.

Lying in calm water behind the reef near Momi and within close proximity to the Nadi International Airport on Viti Levu are more than two dozen islands that belong to the **Mamanuca** group. These paradisiacal isles have long been acknowledged as among the most beautiful in the world. These paradisiacal isles have long been acknowledged among the most beautiful in the world.

There are over 12 island resorts to choose from (see *Practical Information*, page 88–9) but one of the first islands to be developed was **Beachcomber Island**. It was formerly the playground of Fiji-born rancher Dan Costello, whose idea was to gather a boatload of friends on a Friday night, provision adequately with good food and beverages and head for an island to enjoy a weekend of fishing, snorkelling and diving. And when darkness fell, a beachside barbecue would be held.

Sun-drenched beaches

The inevitable soon happened: Costello took a lease on Beachcomber Island, fitted out an old island trader and named it *Ratu Bulumakau* (Chief Bull), and started daily trips to the island. The 1-hour trip included entertainment in the form of a string band and a great deal of good clean fun. To complete the picture, Costello built several *bures* so that people could spend the night, and **Beachcomber Island Resort** was thus born.

Beachcomber Island Resort (tel: 6661500; www.beachcomberfiji.com) is unique among the 12 resorts in the Mamanutha Islands in that it caters to varied tastes, from backpackers who stay in native-style long house dormitories and have buffet meals for an inclusive price, to the young-at-heart who join in the many activities, and retire to the privacy of a secluded *bure* where prices are considerably higher.

Windsurf on transparent waters

These days, the schooner-rigged *Tui Tai* (with bar facilities on board) sails each day from Lautoka's Queen's Wharf for the 70-minute cruise to the island, bringing guests who come to enjoy the ambience the island offers and, for a fee, activities such as windsurfing, hobie cat sailing, snorkelling, scuba diving, fishing and parasailing. At night, there are entertaining shows, parties and dancing barefoot on the sand. If you prefer not to spend the night, book yourself on a day trip instead.

The reputation established by Costello is jealously guarded by him to this day and the routine of so many years ago is still maintained religiously. Most Fridays, Costello boards the *Tui Tai* for the island and spends the weekend there to make sure his guests enjoy themselves — as countless thousands of others have done so before them.

Beachcomber Island Resort

47

The Yasawa Islands, lying like a chain of blue beads in the horizon, are reminiscent of the quintessential South Pacific. The Blue Lagoon cruise presents highlights of these islands.

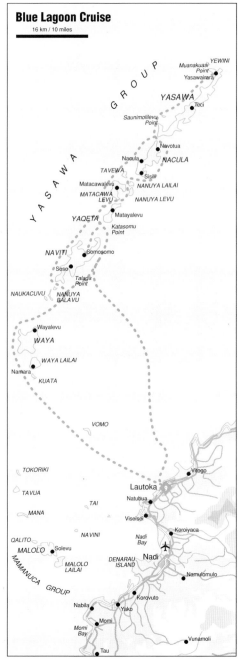

Blue Lagoon Cruise

16 km / 10 miles

GROUP

YEWINI
Muanakuasi
Point
Yasawairara

YASAWA

Teci

Saunimolilevu
Point

Navotua

Naoula NACULA

TAVEWA

Sisili

Matacawalevu NANUYA LAILAI

MATACAWA
LEVU NANUYA LEVU

YAQETA Matayalevu

Katasomu
Point

NAVITI Somosomo

Soso

Talada
Point

NAUKACUVU NANUYA
BALAVU

Wayalevu

WAYA

WAYA LAILAI

Namara

KUATA

VOMO

TOKORIKI Vitogo

Lautoka

TAVUA

TAI Natubua

MANA Viseisei

NAVINI Koroiyaca

QALITO Nadi
MALOLO Solevu Bay Nadi

MALOLO DENARAU
LAILAI ISLAND

MAMANUCA Namulomulo

Korovuto

Nabila Yako

Momi

Momi
Bay

Tau Vunamoli

The words 'blue lagoon' are almost a cliche after three Hollywood movies of the same name portrayed the fantasy of two shipwrecked children cast ashore on a tropical island. Surrounded by nature, they grow to adulthood, find love and happiness and are eventually rescued.

All three movies were shot in Fiji in the **Yasawa Islands**, a group of spectacularly beautiful islands 40km (25 miles) north-west of Lautoka. The first movie, starring Jean Simmons, was filmed in 1948; the re-make in 1979 featured Brooke Shields, and the third movie in 1991, *Return to the Blue Lagoon*, starred Milla Jovovich.

A New Zealand naval officer, the late Trever Withers, helped in the original 1948 production. He had come to Fiji with the famed aviator Harold Gatty to see if there were sufficient tuna in Fijian waters for a major fishery. They spent four years conducting surveys and reluctantly concluded that there was not enough fish, although time was to prove them wrong as Fiji now has a major cannery.

Withers nonetheless fell in love with the Yasawa Islands and its people, and decided to set up **Blue Lagoon Cruises**, borrowing the name from the movie. It seemed like

Jean Simmons, in the original 'Blue Lagoon'

Jean Simmons, in the original 'Blue Lagoon'

a good idea at the time, but he never saw it succeed. After more than 15 years of hard struggle, Withers became ill and sold his interest. But in the period of nearly three decades following that, the company developed an unsurpassed reputation as one of Fiji's leading cruise operators and is one of only two operators to cruise in the waters around the Yasawas.

It took that amount of time for the rest of the world to discover the islands and people that Captain Withers had found.

Blue Lagoon offers several options, all of which begin from Lautoka – a 3-day cruise on the 39-metre (128-ft) *MV Lycianda*; a 4-day cruise on the 54-metre (177-ft) *MV Yasawa Princess*, or on the 56-metre (184-ft) *MV Mystique Princess*; and also a 7-day Gold Club Cruise on the 60-metre (197-ft) *MV Fiji Princess*.

The vessels sail around the 22 beautiful Yasawa Islands with their pristine, sheltered bays and beaches. The cruise itineraries typically

Crystal clear waters and seafood aplenty in the Yasawas

Coral reefs in the lagoon at Naviti Island, Yasawas

include a visit to an island village and a shell and handicraft market, and allow ample time for windsurfing, paddle boarding, snorkelling, spy boarding, swimming or fish-feeding by hand. The cruise schedule usually also includes a visit to Blue Lagoon's private island holding, a 23-hectare (60-acre) plantation on the pristine **Nanuya Lailai** island. While here, guests may experience the *yaqona* ceremony, a *meke* (traditional Fijian song and dance), and a traditional island feast prepared in a *lovo*, or earth oven.

The vessels run through the colourful coral reefs of the Bligh Water to the Yasawa Islands. There are a total of 60 islands stretching in a line for more than 80km (49¾ miles),

Fijian entertainment

most of which are minuscule except for 10 major ones. Most of the islands in the Yasawas group are largely undeveloped. Blue Lagoon's ships weave a magical course between the islands, cruising an average of 4 hours each day to new destinations, usually early in the morning or late in the afternoon, so that there is ample time during the day for guests to spend onshore.

The cruise vessels are manned by a Fijian crew, many of whom come from the Yasawa Islands. The crew members are excellent hosts; easy and friendly without being obsequious or patronising. The Fijians generally regard visitors as honoured guests and take pleasure in caring for them. Depending on the cruise ship you have chosen, accommodation can range from air-conditioned cabins with up to three berths and with attached bathrooms and toilets, to deluxe staterooms with king-size beds and all the amenities of a five-star hotel. Deck cabins usually have windows while lower cabins have port-holes.

The cruise price includes five meals a day: breakfast, lunch and dinner, and morning and afternoon tea with freshly baked cakes and pastries. The menu is varied, with Fijian, Indian and European dishes, complemented by lavish buffets, outdoor beach barbecues of unlimited steaks, salads and fruits, and island theme nights where the food is cooked in underground *lovo*s and accompanied by traditional Fijian entertainment.

Fares start from F$1,000 per person (twin-share cabin) for a 3-day Club Cruise during the low season to as high as F$8,000 per person for a stateroom on a 7-day Gold Club Cruise during the high season. Each boat has several accommodation options with cabins available on different deck levels.

Bookings can be made at tel: 6661622, e-mail: marketing@blc.com.fj or through your travel agent. Check www.bluelagoon cruises.com for more information.

10. Viti Levu Hikes

Ample rewards await adventurers bold enough to leave their air-conditioned hotel rooms and venture into the rugged interior of Fiji. You have the option of either booking a trek with a local agent who will make all the arrangements, or following the recommended 4-day itinerary I have devised.

In 1970, I took a 5-day hike through the interior of **Viti Levu**. My guide at that time was 60-year-old **Ilai Naibose**. We became good friends. I paid his fee, and gave him a donation and plenty of advice on how to start his own business. Thus, Inland Safaris was born. The company Naibose founded is now run by his grandson, who follows his grandfather's philosophy: to take visitors into the bush and show them the 'real' Fiji and the 'real' Fijians. Today, the company is known as **Victory Inland Safaris** (tel: 6700243, e-mail: touristinfofj@connect.com.fj, www.victory.com.fj).

Friendly villagers you will meet on your hike

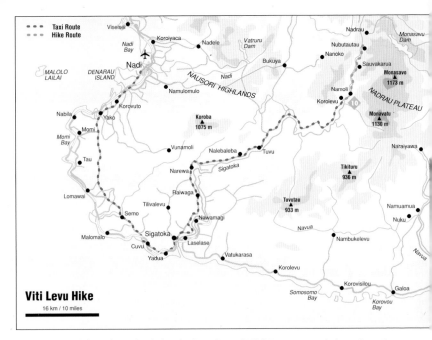

● ● ● Taxi Route
● ● ● Hike Route

Viti Levu Hike

16 km / 10 miles

I have been back in the interior of Viti Levu several times but the memory of that first trip with Naibose is as vivid today as it was when we finished our hike. From Tavua town, we travelled a zigzag road in an old bus up the face of Fiji's highest mountain range to the forestry settlement at Nadarivatu, spending the first night at an elevation of more than 607m (2,000ft) above sea level. The next day, we followed an ancient trail on mountain ridges, through rainforest and across sparkling mountain streams to Navai, and then onto Nadrau, almost in the very heart of the main island.

Early the next morning, we set off on the longest hike of the trip – 10 hours of walking to the village of **Nubutautau**. I had always wanted to see this village because it is famous in Fiji's history as the place where the missionary Reverend Baker was killed and eaten in 1867 – a time when most other parts of Fiji had already accepted Christianity and given up cannibalism. Our first view of the village was through forest giants on a high ridge above the valley.

Interior, Viti Levu

We arrived late in the afternoon, welcomed by the great great grandchildren of the chief who ordered Baker killed, and were even shown the axe with which the blow was struck. Many stories have been offered for Baker's death – the only missionary ever killed by Fijians. According to one version, Baker had a comb which he used in the presence of the chief. The chief asked to see the handsome comb of whalebone, placing it in his hair and thus laying claim to it in the old Fijian custom. Baker, seeing that it was not returned, rose, walked to the chief and took it out of his hair, committing in Fijian eyes the greatest profanity of all as a chief's head is always held sacred by his people. Baker's fate was thus sealed.

The most likely cause of Baker's death, however, was political. A whale's tooth was sent up to Nubutautau by a faction opposed to Christianity. The chief accepted the *tabua* and ordered Baker killed.

The original stonewash

I was taken to the exact spot where Baker fell. A small mound of stones in the shade of tall bamboo was the only memorial of this event. Since then, an act of atonement was performed by the villagers and a small memorial erected. Three days later, we emerged at the Keyasi in the Sigatoka River valley and took a bus back to the coast.

Victory Inland Safaris can arrange tours to this world, beginning from Tavua, depending on how much time you can afford. An 8-day package includes overnight visits to the villages of **Yanuku** and **Navai**, and a hike to the summit of **Mount Tomanivi** (Mount Victoria).

For those who would like to do their own thing, I've devised a special hike. Make sure you are adequately prepared with extra clothes, mosquito nets, insect repellent and a small medical kit, flashlight, food such as corned beef, sugar, tea, rice and flour packed watertight, and packets of cigarettes and money in small denominations. If you like fishing, take a casting rod and lures with you as the rivers are full of bass. A taxi from Nadi up the Sigatoka Valley to Korolevu village at the end of the road will cost approximately F$100 one way. Stop on the way at Sigatoka to purchase your necessary supplies.

If you want to enjoy local flavour and lower cost, 3-ton trucks, equipped with seats depart Sigatoka for Korolevu between 2pm and 4pm each day except Sunday. Buy 1kg (2lb) of lamb chops and fresh bread for the first night; cheese for sandwiches for lunch the following day and 500g (1lb) of *yaqona* (the mildly narcotic root of the piper mythisticum plant) for your *sevusevu* (presentation to the chief). Thereafter you can purchase *yaqona* in each village when you first arrive. Divide your

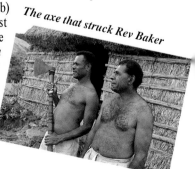

The axe that struck Rev Baker

purchases into daily rations so you can give your host family two cans of corned beef, 1kg (2lb) of flour, rice and sugar, and a packet of tea and sweets for the children. Double the ration if there are two of you. The men will greatly appreciate a packet of cigarettes.

The car journey will take more than 3 hours if you stop to take pictures as you ascend up the valley road. Try and arrive before 2pm so there is plenty of time to make arrangements to spend the night in the village. On arrival at **Korolevu** village ask to see the Turaga ni Koro, the village administrator. Explain that you want to spend the night and then go with him to present your *sevusevu* to the chief. Also explain that you wish to spend a few days up the river on your way to Nubutautau and arrange for someone to go ahead to prepare accommodation at the villages of **Sauvakarua** and **Nubutautau**. Make sure you arrange for a horse to carry your baggage and supplies.

Fishing, Viti Levu

Everything is now set for a most enjoyable time. Although I have done these hikes many times, I still enjoy the evening baths in the river, the fishing and hunting, the huge, tasty meals which in retrospect seem like feasts, and above all, the quiet, measured pace of village life and the open, friendly faces of the people.

As you leave the next day, give your host family F$15 to F$20 for each guest in your group. Allow F$5 per day for your guide and F$5 for the horse. The guide will be a villager who will be only too happy to take you to the next village. Your host family or the Turaga ni Koro will make all the necessary arrangements. Make sure you confirm the fee first. A hard day's trek will take you past the village of **Namoli** to your first destination, **Sauvakarua**.

The next day's trek is shorter and brings you to the infamous **Nubutautau**. For those who have the time, spend 2 days in each village. An overnight at the villages of Korolevu, Sauvakarua and Nubutautau, and back to Sauvakarua and return to Korolevu will take 4 days. Return to Sigatoka on the village truck.

If you wish to explore a different part of Viti Levu, the 25,000-hectare (62,000-acre) **Koroyanitu National Heritage Park** in the Koroyanitu (Mount Evans) range, about 10km (6 miles) south-east of Lautoka, has beautiful nature walks, waterfalls, archaeological sites and good swimming spots.

Call the **Abaca Visitor Centre** (tel: 6666644, dial 1234 after the beep) for details and to make arrangements.

Sauvakarua Village

Savusavu harbour and township

11. Exploring Fiji's North

For those who venture off the beaten track, the north of Fiji offers wonderful rewards and world-class diving. Allow at least a week for a general tour, with stays at resorts and islands along the way. There is no fixed itinerary, instead I've given general directions and recommendations on where to stay. Tailor your exploration of this area according to the amount of time you have.

The 'north' is a general term applied to the islands of Vanua Levu, Taveuni, Qamea, Laucala, Rabi, Kioa, Matangi and the magical Ringold Isles, as well as the coral reefs of Heemskirk, Qelelevu, Wailangilala and Duff. The largest of these islands is **Vanua Levu**, comprising 5,535sq km (2,137sq miles), and is irregular in shape, running on a south-west to north-east axis for approximately 161km (100 miles) and seldom exceeding 48km (30 miles) in width.

As in Viti Levu, there is a mountainous interior which runs the length of the island and is closer to the east coast, where it traps the moisture-laden south-east trade winds and divides the island climatically. The east tends to have much more rain than the west. Sugar cane is grown on the western side and Labasa, which grew up around the sugar mill, rivals Lautoka as Fiji's second largest city after Suva.

Yacht regatta, Savusavu

To get to Vanua Levu, fly to **Savusavu**, the second largest town in Vanua Levu, either from Nadi or Suva. **Sun Air** (tel: 7723016; www.fiji.to) offers two flights daily from Nadi, while **Air Fiji** (tel: 3313666; www.airfiji.com.fj) operates two flights daily from Nadi as well as from Suva. You can also go to Savusavu from Suva by taking the ferry operated by **Beachcomber Cruises** (tel: 3307889; www.beachcomberfiji.com), which has regular services several times a week.

Savusavu is on the eastern coast of Vanua Levu, occupying a strategic position in the middle of the island. The township nestles around a beautiful natural harbour

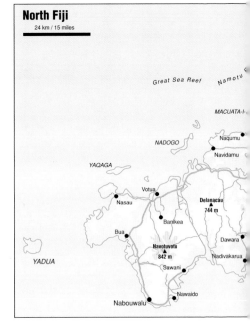

North Fiji

24 km / 15 miles

and is a major port of entry to Fiji. The commercial centre hugs a narrow coastal strip beside the harbour. **Nawi Island** is immediately offshore and the deep water between the island and the town is a perfect anchorage for visiting yachts. Near the wharf are some hot springs, a reminder that **Savusavu Bay** was once a volcanic caldera. One of Savusavu's attractions are its spectacular dive sites.

The road follows the bay towards the **Lesiaceva Point** stretch, where there are a number of resorts. The upmarket **Jean-Michel Cousteau Fiji Islands Resort** (tel: 415-7885794; www.fijiresort.com) features a reception and dining area in the style of a *bure kalou* (ancient temple) and accommodation *bure*s tucked among coconut trees and flowering bougainvillea.

Bure-style Jean-Michel Consteau Resort

The main road runs northeast over the hill and along the coast, passing the **Namale Resort and Spa** (tel: 8850435; www.namalefiji.com). It is tucked away on a small peninsula with a white sandy beach. An atmosphere of tranquillity is fostered through the lush landscaping and by limiting the number of guests to a maximum of 20 at any one time. Resort guests are accommodated in 10 *bure*s featuring traditional thatch roofs, exquisite interiors and private decks with spectacular views. The resort also offers extensive spa services as well as a full range of activities.

The **Hibiscus Highway** between Savusavu and Buca Bay attracts

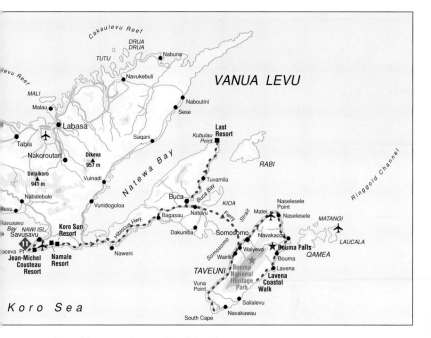

people seeking an alternative lifestyle. For some reason, North Americans in particular seem drawn to this part of Fiji. A short distance along the road from the **Koro Sun Resort** (tel: 8850262; www.korosunresort.com), the late US Air Force Colonel Gordon Edris built a small hotel called **Mumu's Place** (tel: 8850416), open to visitors seeking budget accommodation.

It is some 60km (37¼ miles) from Savusavu to **Buca Bay** along this scenic highway, while another road turns left 3km (1¾ miles) past the Koro Sun Resort to join **Natewa Bay**, continuing for 130km (81 miles) in a grand sweep around the bay, crossing the mountains and eventually reaching **Labasa**, the largest town in Vanua Levu.

The main road continues on past the Natuvu turn-off (the ferry point to Taveuni) to its terminal at Napuka, passing the **Tuvamila** estate, owned by the late Laurie Simpson, son of local self-made millionaire David Simpson and his wife Dorothy. Further along, a group of alternative lifestyle Americans purchased a property at **Kubulau**, just before the end of the road, and called it the **Last Resort**. Sadly, it never achieved its ambition as a budget guesthouse and is now minded by a caretaker.

Two islands offshore, **Rabi** and **Kioa**, are home to different communities. Rabi was purchased for the Banaba (Ocean Island) people, whose home was mined for phosphate. Royalties from the sale of phosphate paid for this island, while the smaller Kioa was purchased on behalf of the people of Tuvalu, who were given the island in recognition of their work with the US armed forces in the war against Japan.

The Simpsons of Tuvamila

The abandoned Last Resort

A daily bus service from Savusavu departs at 10am and reaches **Natuvu** at 1pm, in time to connect with a small ferry for the 2-hour trip to **Waiyevo** on the island of **Taveuni**. It is a scenic drive with local flavour and to me offers more than a brief plane hop to Taveuni or the ferry trip from Savusavu to Taveuni. If you plan to do just Taveuni and skip Vanua Levu, there is a direct flight from Suva and another one via Savusavu from Nadi.

Taveuni is Fiji's third largest island and geologically, its most recent. It is of volcanic origin and known as the 'garden isle' for its large tracts of rainforest and a profusion of bird life.

The 180th longitude meridian, or International Dateline, passes through Taveuni at a point slightly west of Waiyevo, and in theory, it is possible to straddle this line so that one foot will be in the 'today' zone and the other in 'yesterday'. However, for practical purposes, this distinction is ignored.

Soon after crossing the dateline, you reach the settlement of **Wairiki**, dominated by a Catholic church and a cross on the hill. This marks the place where the hitherto undefeated forces of the Tongan chief Ma'afu suffered a decisive loss against the Tui Cakau.

Taveuni once attracted European planters and some estates here are owned by their descendants. About 3km (1¾ miles) south of Wairiki, the **Soqulu estate** was part of an ambitious American development scheme. Blocks of land were sold and a number of people built houses in the rainforest on the hillside overlooking **Somosomo Strait**. Despite the magnificent views, the development never realised its full potential.

It is 20km (12½ miles) south from Waiyevo to **Vuna** and an additional 7km (4¼ miles) to **South Cape**. The drive north-east from

A copra plantation

Waiyevo is equally spectacular. The road will pass the settlement and village of **Somosomo**, seat of the Tui Cakau (Lord of the Reef), paramount chief of the province of Cakaudrove. The current incumbent, Ratu Sir Penaia Ganilau, was a former President of Fiji. It continues along the coast to **Naselesele Point** and the airport at **Matei**, and then bears to the south-east to reveal a colourful lagoon dotted with the larger islands of Qamea and Laucala. A number of places offer accommodation near the airport.

Navakacoa landing, 8km (5 miles) from the airport, is the pick-up point for

Spear dance, Somosomo Village

the islands of Qamea, Laucala and Matangi. Each island has a resort hotel. **Laucala** was purchased by publishing tycoon, the late Malcolm Forbes, who turned it into a private playground and willed his remains to be interred on the island.

One very attractive resort is the **Matangi Island Resort** (tel: 8880260; www.matangiisland.com), a 97-hectare (240-acre) copra plantation with 11 beachfront *bures* operated by the Douglas family. The private island lies 10km (6¼ miles) from Navakacoa landing, and is located beside a beautiful white-sand beach facing **Qamea** island with a blue lagoon between. The family-run resort is limited to 24 guests at any one time and operates two live-aboard dive vessels, taking full advantage of superb diving and cruising. The opposite side of the island is where the famous **Horse Shoe Bay** and beach are located.

Situated away from the big resorts and some 7km (4¼ miles) from Navakacoa landing is the **Bouma National Heritage Park**. Encompassing approximately 15,000 hectares (58sq miles) of rainforest and coastal forest, the park is actually private land owned by the villages of Waitabu, Vidawa, Korovou and Lavena. The area consists of several kilometres of bush walks and three beautiful waterfalls with natural swimming pools. Treks range between 15 minutes to 2 hours return. Refreshments, food and information are available at the **Bouma Visitor Centre** (tel: 8880390), which is situated at the entrance to the falls.

One of the best hiking experiences on Taveuni must be the **Lavena Coastal Walk**, which begins at Lavena village, about 15 minutes' drive past Bouma. Allow at least 3 hours return for the

Matangi Island's Horse Shoe Bay

wild and beautiful walk on a flat and well maintained track that snakes along the southeastern coastline of Taveuni. This 5-km (3-mile) route eventually leads to the stunning **Wainabau Falls**, which is situated within a natural amphitheatre. To reach the falls, a short swim through two deep pools is required, so take your swimwear and a waterproof camera. More information can be obtained from the **Lavena Visitor Centre** (tel: 8880453).

As with other Fijian inhabitants, the villagers at Bouma and Lavena lead conservative lifestyles, so be sure to dress modestly and refrain from skinny-dipping.

12. Toberua Island Resort

A number of small and super exclusive resorts in Fiji, some with private beaches to frolic on and prices to match, guarantee a sinfully self-indulgent experience.

Fiji's 300 islands offer something for everyone, and resorts have been built to cater for varying tastes and budgets, from those of lavish multi-millionaires to penny-pinching backpackers. **Toberua Island**, tucked away among a maze of coral reefs in Fiji's Bau Waters between the mainland of Viti Levu and the island of Ovalau, and several others such as the luxurious **Wakaya**, **Vatulele**, **Turtle Island** and **Yasawa** resorts (see *Practical Information*, pages 89–90), are in a category and class apart.

The marketing strategy of these resorts is simple: Cater to a small number of guests and pamper them to the hilt. Some, like **Kaimbu** in northern Lau, are so exclusive that there are only three luxurious cottages, each with its own private beach, and a rate of well over US$1,000 a day for two.

Reef golf at Toberua at low tide

Toberua Fiji Luxury Resort (tel: 3302356; www.toberua.com) is a gem. This tiny island of 1.6ha (4 acres) is a miniature botanic garden with 15 guest *bures* built by Fijian craftsmen in a style that honours their highest chiefs. Children are welcome at this resort.

Toberua was one of the first in Fiji to see the need for a small exclusive island resort and set about creating the conditions and ambience that would appeal to the discerning up-market traveller. Toberua does not only provide luxurious accommodation and superior cuisine – many places in the world can do this – but it has also succeeded in creating an atmosphere where the unique nature of the island, the Fijian staff and the culture of the people in nearby villages have

A beach to call your own

melded harmoniously. Guests may begin their adventure from the **Nakelo** landing beside an old trading post on the **Navualoa River**, in the heart of Viti Levu's Rewa River delta, which lies a few minutes from Suva's Nausori International Airport. The 40-minute boat ride down the river is a fantastic way to begin the holiday.

The island is within sight of some of Fiji's most historic landmarks. To the north-west is the island of **Bau**, the seat of Fiji's highest chiefs; to the south-west the **Kaba Peninsula** where Fiji's last great battle was fought; to the north-east, the island of **Ovalau** and the old capital, **Levuka**.

The daily programme includes many options – even playing golf on the reef at low tide! Besides the usual assortment of watersports like hobie cat sailing and windsurfing, there are fishing trips and scuba diving excursions for certified divers, and of course, snorkelling. For nature lovers, the resort can arrange complimentary boat trips to nearby locations, including the **Nasamila Mangrove Forest and Picnic Island** with its uninhabited white sand cays, where you can enjoy a full day's snorkelling, swimming and sun-bathing. For a fee, you may also take a trip to nearby Levuka, the former capital of Fiji (see pages 38–39).

Understandably, paradise comes at a high price: Toberua Fiji Luxury Resort's packages cost at least F$690 per person a day for accommodation, food and beverages, as well as transfers to and from the island. As with many resorts, Toberua Island is an ideal location for a wedding. The resort offers a wedding package for up to 30 guests, and ensures complete privacy.

Toberua Island lies among a maze of reefs in the Bau Waters

Activities

13. Scuba Diving and Snorkelling

Fjii has some of the best dive sites in the world. The secret is out now, and there are more than 60 dive operators offering their services, including certification courses. The water is both warm and clear, and divers will find a profusion of tropical hard and soft corals, as well as an array of fish – including sharks – in a bewildering kaleidoscope of colours and shapes. Look out also for a stunning variety of caves, overhangs, mazes, walls and drop-offs. One of the attractions of scuba diving in Fiji is the great variety of marine life the waters offer. The names of some of the famous dive sites suggest their diversity: Blue Ribbon Eel Reef, The Ledge, Fish Factory Corner, Cabbage Patch, Korolevu, Jack's Place, Yellow Tunnel, Barracuda Hole, Small White Wall, Annie's Bommie and The Zoo.

There are amazing underwater experiences to be had: take for example the Great White Wall of Taveuni, where you enter a tunnel at a depth of 9m (30ft) and exit at 27½m (90ft) on the face of a vertical wall covered with a profuse growth of soft white coral as far as the eye can see. Patrolling the face of the wall is an abundance of multi-coloured fish, so tame that they brush fearlessly against you. Next, you ascend to 17m (55ft) and enter another tunnel which takes you to the top of the reef at 11m (35ft).

Colourful reefs and clear waters make Fiji a top dive spot

There are a several resorts catering for divers. These offer courses and trips with full equipment, and are invariably located near the best dive sites. Some of these sites are **Beqa Island**, **Kadavu Island** and **Astrolabe Lagoon**, **Wakaya Island**, **Savusavu Barrier Reef**, **Namenalala Island**, and **Taveuni**, **Matagi**, **Qamea** and **Laucala** islands.

The best times to dive are the dry winter months from May to October when the water visibility usually exceeds 30m (98 ft). An itinerary can be arranged to dive at a number of different locations or on a live-aboard dive boat. Two well-reputed local dive operators are **Sea Fiji Travel** (tel: 6520751, www.seafiji.com) and **Subsurface Fiji** (tel: 6666738, www.subsurfacefiji.com). **Fiji Visitors Bureau** provides details of other operators on its its website, www.bulafiji.com.

Non-divers can snorkel instead. Viewing areas can come close to prime scuba-diving sites. Colourful soft corals and fish can be seen while you snorkel over shallow reefs, close to shore. One place among many is **Nananu-i-ra**, a beautiful island off the coast from Rakiraki. It has a 'skinny' middle you can walk across in minutes, giving you access to two beaches where the snorkelling is fantastic.

14. Fishing

Fishing in Fiji appeals to different preferences. There is deep-sea game or sport fishing for fish such as striped, black or blue marlin, sailfish, yellowfin, dog-tooth tuna, shark, wahoo, giant trevally and mahimahi (dolphin fish). There is also fishing for ground fish which the whole family can enjoy in the shelter of the lagoon, and there is fishing from the shore, where the angler casts his lure among patches of coral to hook powerful tropical trevallys, barracuda, queenfish, coral trout and the Spanish mackerel. Finally, there is the art of fly fishing for the wily bonefish on tidal flats.

Apart from sea fishing, Fiji's rivers also thrive with freshwater varieties waiting to be hooked. The rivers are home to large mouth bass and it is possible to drive to remote and beautiful places for a day's fishing, or to make arrangements to hire a punt or an inflatable raft to drift downstream while casting for fish.

Many resort hotels include game fishing as part of the optional activities available to guests. Some of the resorts own and operate their own fishing boats; others operate boats in association with sub-contracting companies.

Fishing for wahoo during Fiji's peak season from July to October is as good as, if not better than, in Hawaii. Fiji's wahoo average 25kg (55lb), but fish twice that weight are also caught. Walu or tanguige (Spanish mackerel and a close cousin to

A good catch

the wahoo) are most plentiful in February. Fiji has blue and black marlin and sometimes striped marlin but not many sailfish, though they are caught regularly.

Prices for a day's deep sea fishing in Fiji depend on the type of boat hired. Top boats cost more than F$1,200 for a full day inclusive of meals. Lesser boats begin at about F$500 and local punts for less than F$100 for some good lagoon fishing. Two well-reputed game fishing operators are: **Xtasea Charters** (tel: 3450280, e-mail: info@xtaseacharters.com) and **Bay Water Charters** (tel: 3450573, e-mail: baywater@connect.com.fj). Otherwise, look up the Fiji Visitors Bureau website (www.bulafiji.com) for more information.

15. Kayaking

If you want a unique Fiji experience, consider doing an exciting whitewater trip on the **Wainikoroiluva River**, located on the upper reaches of the Namosi Valley. Operated by **Rivers Fiji** (tel: 3450147, fax: 3450148, e-mail: info@riversfiji.com, www.riversfiji.com), the trip is an adventure for both the body and soul.

The day begins with an ascent into the highlands through beautiful virgin rainforests and over mountain passes offering spectacular panoramic views of the mist-shrouded Namosi valley, with occasional glimpses of the silver braids of the river far below. The only sound you will hear once your vehicle has stopped is the relentless chorus of native birds.

The drive from from the town of **Navua** to **Nakavika** village on the banks of the Wainikoroiluva River takes more than an hour. At the launch point, the kayaks will be inflated and your guide will give you a crash course on the basics of kayaking and some safety tips. After donning life-vests and safety helmets, the single-paddler kayaks are put into the river for the first stage which takes you down the river through rock mazes and whitewater rapids. Once

Exhilarating ride on the Wainikoroiluva River

your confidence grows, shooting the Class II rapids and navigating through rock mazes becomes less daunting, allowing you more time to enjoy the magnificent surroundings. There is also time on this leg of the journey to take a rejuvenating 'shower' beneath one of the many waterfalls, stop for a delicious picnic lunch in a garden grotto and soak up the beauty of this unspoiled wilderness.

Negotiating rock chasms

The ride ends at Namuamua village, 10km (6 miles) downriver, where you board motorised long boats for the trip down the rest of the river to Navua. The first part is through a gorge with rainforests on each side clinging tenaciously to the rock faces. Cascading waterfalls await at virtually every turn. This last stage of 23km (14 miles) brings you to Navua township in just over an hour to connect with your transport for the trip back to your hotel.

Note: If the thought of handling single-paddler kayaks does not appeal to you, Rivers Fiji also operates rafting trips on the Upper Navua River in inflatable rafts for up to six people.

16. Surfing

Fiji has been acknowledged as having some of the best surfing spots in the world. Several outstanding locations for surfing on Viti Levu include **Cloudbreak** and **Restaurants**, on the west of Viti Levu; the **Sand Dunes** near the mouth of the Sigatoka River, **Natadola Beach** with its challenging 'outside' reef break and several stretches along the **Coral Coast**, including near the Hideaway Resort and Waidroka Bay. Outside of Viti Levu is the famous **Frigate Passage**, on the Beqa Island barrier reef, where Fiji's best breaks can be found. Away from Viti Levu but still within striking distance are the islands of **Tavarua** and **Namotu**, which are well known with the international surfing community. There are two dedicated surfing camps on **Beqa Island** and **Yanuca Island**, but you can just as easily charter a surf board, in Nadi, from **Fiji Surf Shop** (tel: 6705960, e-mail: fijisurf@connect.com.fj; www.fijisurfshop.com).

Further out, 100km (62¼ miles) south of the main island of Viti Levu, is Fiji's fourth largest island, **Kadavu**, with its proximity to the **Great Astrolabe Reef**. Linked by air from both Nadi and Nausori airports, the island is a popular destination for outstanding surfing, in addition to good diving and fishing.

There are many other surf hot spots in the Fijian archipelago, but they are more difficult to access. Note: the best surfing season is the dry winter months from May to October when huge breaks are caused by the low pressure system.

Shopping

Shopping in Fiji falls into several categories. There is a local market that caters to the very different needs of indigenous Fijians and Indian migrants who also form a large part of the population. Many of the differences between the two races and their cultures are reflected in the personal items, food and jewellery they purchase. There is also a thriving market for visitors that offers duty-free electronic goods, watches, cameras, perfumes, gold and brand-name products from Europe and Asia. Fijian handicrafts and artefacts are the final category and these range from well-executed traditional items to carvings and gift items made especially for the tourist trade.

Handicrafts and Souvenirs

Handicrafts and artefacts include well-made replicas of old weapons, cannibal forks, wooden bowls used for ritual purposes and for serving *yaqona,* mats, fans and baskets woven out of pandanus, pottery and *masi* (also known as *tapa*), a type of bark cloth. It's illegal to take out *tabua* (sperm whale teeth) which are of great ritual value in Fiji. Do not buy turtle-shell or whalebone products, either –

One of the many duty-free shops that line Suva town

they will be confiscated by customs officials if you are returning to the United States.

One 500-year-old clay pot was recently found, but rarely are these in mint condition as most antiques are made of wood and therefore prone to the ravages of time. The Fiji Museum in Suva (see *Pick and Mix*, page 30) has a fine collection of antiques as do some of the old European families, but the museum certainly won't part with theirs and visitors are unlikely to find families willing to sell their heirlooms.

Two common local handicrafts are *masi* and *pandanus* mats. *Masi*, also known as *tapa*, is a thick bark cloth with black and rust-coloured painted designs that is traditionally used for births, deaths and other ceremonial occasions. Woven *pandanus*-leaf mats are used in homes as floor coverings, dining mats and sleeping mats, and are much in demand as wedding presents, for baptisms and funerals, and as presentations to chiefs.

In Suva, the official government crafts centre at **Ratu Sukuna House** has some fine items. The Suva outlets, especially the government store, tend to be a little expensive but the quality is quite good. Most of the city's best shops are along Victoria Parade and on Cumming Street. The largest merchants are **Prouds**, which is located at the triangle near the Fiji Visitors Bureau and at the corner of Thomson and Cumming streets; **Tappoo**, which can be found at the corner of Thomson and Usher streets; and Jack's Handicrafts, which you will see at Thomson and Pier streets, opposite the Fiji Visitors Bureau.

Jacks Handicrafts (tel: 6700744; www.jacksfiji.com) is the largest retailer in the South Pacific with 12 outlets around the islands, including a downtown Nadi store located just 15 minutes away from Nadi International Airport. The shops offer a wide array of products,

Curio shops and woodcrafts

ranging from printed garments, such as t-shirts and tapa cloth, to traditional South Pacific art, souvenirs, unusual jewellery, and other gift items.

Those interested in replicas of original artefacts and antiques should first go to the **Fiji Museum** (Government Buildings, Thurston Gardens, tel: 3315944, e-mail: info@fijimuseum.org.fj) and carefully examine the relics there. These are the models for the reproductions you are buying. The aforementioned museum has a small but comprehensive gift shop.

Most of the municipal markets in the larger towns such as Suva, Nadi and Lautoka have large handicraft sections.

Electronic Goods

There are scores of duty-free shops selling cameras, electronic equipment and perfumes in Suva, Nadi and Lautoka. For top quality hi-fidelity equipment try **Maneklal's** at 141 Vitogo Parade, Lautoka, tel: 6665242, or its branch at the Honson Arcade, Thomson Street, Suva, tel: 3305384. Maneklal's imports the best brand names and offers a selection of top-of-the-line equipment at good prices. These are generally between 10 and 20 percent lower than in most other countries, depending on the product. Do not be taken in by individual hustlers frequenting these areas who will offer to get you goods for an even lower price.

Municipal Markets

Each town has a municipal market which opens early in the morning and closes at 5pm. These are always colourful and especially so on Friday and Saturday mornings when the markets are at their busiest with vendors spilling onto the footpaths and even the roads. Fresh vegetables, root crops, seasonal fruit such as avocado, pineapple, mango, papaya and banana, spices essential for Indian cuisine, piles of dried *yaqona* and local tobacco cured into coils are usually on display.

Yaqona (piper mysthisticum) roots are pounded into powder and mixed with water to produce a mildly narcotic drink to which most of the population, both Fijian and Indian, are extremely partial to. *Yaqona* has an important ritual significance in Fijian culture. An elaborate ceremony surrounds its presentation, preparation and serving. Visitors will have many opportunities to taste it. A slight numbing of the lips is the immediate effect. It takes a great deal of *yaqona* (imbibing over several hours) to produce a mildly euphoric state. Regular drinkers of the drink are said to experience a quicker response.

Municipal markets offer the best opportunity for absorbing the local scene. Suva has the largest (see *Pick & Mix* page 30). You can stand to one side with a slice of fresh pineapple or melon in hand and watch the press of people without feeling that you're intruding.

Shopping Tips

Shops are usually open Mondays to Fridays from 8am to 5pm and Saturdays from 8am to 3pm.

A word of caution: It can be fun strolling down the streets of Nadi, Lautoka or Suva. The air is usually heavy with the smell of incense, loud Hindi music and the aroma of spicy foods. Sometimes the Indian shopkeepers can be over enthusiastic with their 'g'day mate!' greetings in their bid to try and get customers into

Municipal market, Suva

Cassava for sale

their stores. Most visitors take it in their stride but some find it annoying. Note also that many duty-free prices may not be as low as those at your regular discount stores back home. In general, electrical goods here are cheaper than in Australia, but more expensive than in the United States.

Beware of Fijians who seem eager to make friends, especially the so-called 'sword sellers'. Most Fijians are genuinely friendly and it is so disarming that most visitors to Suva, Nadi and Lautoka fall easy prey to the 'sword sellers' who trade on it. This scam is especially successful around ports of entry and airports before visitors are familiar with their surroundings. The ploy is very simple: a 'sword seller' will first make friends with a cheery 'bula!' or 'hello, mate!' and then proceed with inquiries about your family and country of origin. He will finally ask your name while at the same time fish out a piece of wood in the shape of a sword and start carving your name on it, and then demand an exorbitant sum for this piece of junk. If you should happen to meet one of these rascals on the streets, just walk away. Just keep walking no matter what he says. Do not look back. If necessary, walk into the nearest store and ask the shopkeeper to call the police. There is nothing he can do and you will save yourself a great deal of anguish. Beware also of 'guides' who promise to take you to shops where you will get the 'best' bargains. Many an overeager tourist has been soundly fleeced by these professional hustlers, even to the point of buying, say, computers that are no more than a shell in a box.

Shell and handicraft market

It is difficult to counsel visitors whether to haggle over prices or not. In formal shops, prices are usually fixed. Elsewhere, the Indians, who own or control many of the shops and market stalls, believe that bargaining is an essential element of shopping. You are expected to haggle over the price of the object that catches your interest. However, once you have begun this process, considerable firmness is required to get out of the shop without buying it. On the other hand, Fijian vendors are averse to bargaining and will be slightly miffed if you try to do so.

Eating Out

Fiji's multi-racial mix is well reflected in the array of cuisines available. Here you will find European food (with a French bias) prepared by leading chefs in the major resorts; Chinese (predominantly Cantonese); Indian with its emphasis on chillies and spices; ethnic Fijian; and a blending of various styles so that a smorgasbord presentation may include some of each.

Fijian Cuisine

The late Ratu Sir Edward Cakobau, as a guest at the Captain's table on his way to England, was clearly not amused when questioned about Fiji's cannibal past. He solemnly studied the menu for some time, turned to the waiter and without batting an eyelid replied: 'The menu does not appear very interesting. Could you please bring me the passenger list?'

Man-eating jokes aside, Fijian cuisine relies on fresh food, cooked simply, usually by boiling. Coconut cream, pressed from the shredded flesh of the nut, is either added during the cooking process or served as a sauce. When the cream is added during cooking, it is called *lolo*; when used as a sauce, it is known as *miti*.

Sunday is always a feast day as in biblical times. Fijians are Christians and punctilious about observing the Sabbath. This day is

Sunday lunch after church

reserved for worship and family get-togethers around a midday feast immediately after church service. Economic circumstances determine the food that is served, but even in villages where money is scarce, the number of dishes will nevertheless be impressive: fresh fish, shellfish, seaweed and *beche de mer* (sea cucumber) from the lagoon, various root crops and vegetables, chicken and sometimes meat, and for dessert, cakes and puddings made from bananas and

Placing food in a lovo

papayas, and fresh fruit. Often there will also be a Fijian version of chop suey and curry. Another local favourite is *kokoda* (fresh, cubed fish marinated in lemon juice and coconut cream), served with hot chilli peppers.

The *lovo* is a Pacific Islands speciality and an ingenious way of cooking food. A pit is dug and lined with river stones. The stones are set on fire, with more stones placed on top of pieces of wood. The size of the pit and of the stones will depend on the amount of food to be cooked. It may be as large as a small swimming pool where a mountain of food will be cooked, including whole pigs, turtles, fish, beef, chicken, root crops and vegetables. In former times this was also the principal means of cooking human flesh.

The fire is allowed to die down and the unburnt pieces and embers are removed and the stones levelled. Green mid-ribs of coconut fronds are placed over the hot stones and food, wrapped in leaves but more often in foil, is placed on the sticks so that the food will not come into direct contact with the stones. Banana leaves and sacking are used to cover the pit and soil is heaped over the *lovo* to trap the heat inside. Two hours later, the 'oven' is opened and the food is ready to be served. Most hotels and resorts feature *lovo* nights accompanied by Fijian entertainment.

Recommendations

Apart from restaurants recommended in the itineraries, the following are some of my personal favourites. Invariably, the best food is served at the best hotels. The two **Sheraton** resorts at Denarau Island, Nadi, each have a number of restaurants

Live crabs ready for the pot

which serve Fijian, Indian, Chinese and European dishes as well as buffets and *lovo* meals.

Prices depend on the restaurant but can be up to F$50 for a main course, though it is possible to have an evening meal for less than F$20. The average price for a three-course dinner for one person without drinks is categorised as follows: Expensive = F$30 and above; Moderate = F$21–$29; Inexpensive = F$20 and below.

Nadi

BOUNTY BAR & RESTAURANT
Queen's Road, Martintar, near airport
Tel: 6720840
The menu features a daily special, as well as good hamburgers and *palusame* (fish with coconut milk). Candle-lit atmosphere and live music. *Moderate*

CHEF'S RESTAURANT
Sagayam Road
Tel: 6703131
Excellent food is served here, along with attentive service. Restaurant opened by two former Sheraton chefs, hence the name. Varied menu featuring *pakapaka* (snapper), seafood, grilled lamb and beef. Lunch and dinner. *Expensive*

DAIKOKU JAPANESE RESTAURANT
Main Street opposite bridge
Tel: 6703622
The Daikoku claims world-class steak and seafood as part of its menu. Teppan-yaki individually prepared at your Teppan table as well as standard classic Japanese cuisine such as sukiyaki, shabu shabu, sashimi etc. There is also a sushi bar. Lunch Monday to Saturday 11.30am–2pm and dinner daily 6–10pm. *Moderate* to *Expensive*

HAMACHO JAPANESE RESTAURANT
Sheraton Royal Denarau Resort
Tel: 6750177
Genuine Japanese cuisine prepared by two Japanese chefs. Try the value-for-money set dinner. Lunch and dinner. Open daily 5.30 to 10pm. *Moderate*

SHERATON FIJI RESORT
Denarau Island
Tel: 6701777
Five excellent restaurants in this five-star hotel to choose from:

PORTS OF CALL
Dinner only. *Expensive*

MALOLO RESTAURANT
Dinner only. *Expensive*

VERANDAH
A sumptuous buffet is served for breakfast, lunch and dinner. *Moderate*

OCEAN LANAI
Lunch and dinner. *Inexpensive*

THE CAFE
Light meals from 10am to 10pm. Good food well presented in very pleasant surroundings. *Inexpensive*

SHERATON ROYAL DENARAU RESORT
Denarau Island
Tel: 6750000
Choose from among these three restaurants:

GARDEN VIEW
Dinner only. *Expensive*

STEAK HOUSE
Lunch and dinner. Superb salad bar. *Moderate* to *Expensive*

OCEAN TERRACE
Breakfast and dinner. The Swiss chef commands a select group of local and expatriate chefs who whip up excellent meals. *Expensive*

TATA'S CURRY RESTAURANT
Back Road opposite Vinod Patel
Tel: 6700502

Typical South Indian home cooking; the curries come especially recommended. *Inexpensive*

WET MONGOOSE
Denarau Marina, Denarau
Tel: 6750900
A popular meeting place for yachtsmen and visitors, this restaurant is run by Cardo, formerly of Main Street, Nadi. There is a bar and a spacious verandah, with seating for outdoor dining views of marina activities. *Expensive*

Lautoka

CYBER ZONE NETCAFÉ
159 Vitogo Parade
Tel: 6651675
Cheap but excellent curries – which some regard as the best in Fiji – and takeaways. Also serves Chinese dishes. Open from 6am to 8pm daily, except Sundays. *Inexpensive*

FIRST LANDING
Vuda Point (next to Vuda Marina)
Tel: 6666171
This is a popular restaurant serving excellent cuisine. Open from 9.30am till midnight, the company also runs **The Hatch Café** (see next column) at the Vuda Marina. *Moderate*

THE HATCH CAFÉ
Vuda Marina (10 minutes from town)
Tel: 6666171
Breakfast is served from 7am, and lunch and snacks until 5pm. Lovely marina setting and good inexpensive food, including Chinese meals, make this a good dining place. *Inexpensive*

Suva

Many new restaurants and bars have opened in Suva in the past few years.

ASHIYANA
Victoria Parade, Old Town Hall
Tel: 3313000
This is the best little Indian restaurant around, with fiery vegetable curries and delicious *naan* breads. *Moderate*

BAD DOG CAFE
219 Victoria Parade
Tel: 3312455
Open for breakfast throughout the day to dinner. Varied menu and nice atmosphere. Part of a complex which also runs the Irish **Wolfhound** and **O'Rielly's** bars, and **Lucky Eddie's** nightclub. Wolfhound and O'Reilly's are the only bars serving Guiness Stout and Kilkenny's beer in Fiji. *Moderate*

CASTLE RESTAURANT
6 Fenton Street, Lami
Tel: 3361223
Good Cantonese food in pleasant surroundings. Open daily for lunch and dinner except Sunday. *Inexpensive*

LANTERN PALACE
10 Pratt Street
Tel: 3314633
Consistenly good Cantonese food makes this one of the most popular restaurants in town. Lunch and dinner is served daily except on Sundays. *Inexpensive*

MALT HOUSE BREWERY & RESTAURANT
88 Jerusalem Road
Tel: 3371515
It is well worth the taxi fare to see this noisy South Seas beer hall with good food, including beef schnitzel, pork cutlets and wood-fired pizzas. *Moderate*

McDONALD'S
Victoria Parade
Tel: 6701474
Yes, even in Fiji the kids love it. Needs no introduction. *Inexpensive*

Victoria Parade from the Queensland Arcade to the **Golden Dragon** nightclub has turned into a restaurant and nightclub strip – recommended:

FONG LEE SEAFOOD RESTAURANT
Tel: 3304233
Inexpensive

DAIKOKU JAPANESE RESTAURANT
Tel: 3308968
Moderate to *Expensive*

HAI KONG SEAFOOD
Tel: 3313988
Inexpensive

PALM COURT BISTRO
17 QI Centre
Tel: 3304662
Attractive outdoor setting in a courtyard with tall palms. The restaurant is located only 20m (22yds) off busy Victoria Parade. Excellent sandwich bar, snacks, light meals and espresso coffee at reasonable prices. Open Mondays to Saturdays for breakfast through to afternoon tea. *Inexpensive*

PIZZA HUT
207 Victoria Parade
Tel: 3311825
Tasty pizza and pasta dishes. Open daily for lunch and dinner except on Sunday when it is open only for dinner from 7pm. *Inexpensive*

THE GREAT WOK OF CHINA
Corner of Bau Street &
Laucala Bay Road
Tel: 3301285
Sichuan food, well prepared and served in pleasant surroundings. Lunch and dinner daily except Sunday. *Moderate*

OLD MILL COTTAGE
49 Carnarvon Street
Tel: 3312134
A must-see, tucked away from the city centre towards the government buildings, but it is worth the walk. This is the only restaurant in Suva serving Fijian, Indian, European and Chinese dishes. The food is good. Open daily for breakfast and lunch except on Sundays. *Moderate*

TIKOS FLOATING RESTAURANT
Stinson Parade
Tel: 3313626
Steak and seafood are served in a former cruise boat moored off Stinson Parade. The restaurant is open daily for lunch and dinner except on Sundays. *Expensive*

Nightlife

The kind of nightlife you look for in Fiji will depend on how dangerously you wish to live. A drunk is a drunk and can either be a nuisance or a menace. Fiji is a small place and the choice of places to go to at night are limited. There is no national orchestra, no ballet and no theatre. Most large hotels have resident bands and discos and in these places you are likely to see more of other tourists and very few locals. Keep an eye on your beer mug. Bartenders in Fiji are taught to keep your beer mug full and your pockets empty – that is, they don't ask if you want another beer, and will keep filling your glass until you emphatically tell them to stop.

Locally-brewed beer

COLD BEER

On the other hand, nightclubs which cater mainly for locals can sometimes become volatile, as excitement, fanned by loud music, drinks and the presence of pretty girls can have unpredictable effects on village boys, often resulting in either fist fights or riots.

Some nightclubs in Fiji will continue until the early hours of the morning, or as long as there is a large crowd present; and there is one in Suva which remains open until dawn, and is, naturally, the gathering place for those who want to continue the party. The exception is Saturday when all clubs are supposed to close at the stroke of midnight because of the Sunday Observance Decree. In practice, this rarely happens. Most visitors, however, opt to have a special meal followed by a Fijian *meke* show (traditional dance); these are available at the main hotels. Traditional Fijian dance re-enacts stories and legends from village folklore. The movements are gentle, even subtle, and are accompanied by a chanting chorus.

Nadi

In the Nadi area, the **Planters Club** (tel: 6701777) at the Sheraton Royal Denarau Resort stands out. Apart from hotel guests, you are

Hotels often feature entertainment from Polynesia

likely to find quite a few of the local people enjoying the ambience. The atmosphere is lively and the security is tight. The barmen are competent at mixing drinks and dance behind the bar while serving customers. The best nights are Fridays and Saturdays when the locals arrive in large numbers.

When the action proves too hot, it is nice to step out and cool off on the edge of one of the pools in the foyer or stroll to the swimming pool near the beach. The **Malolo Lounge**, next to the Planters Club, features a resident band and a more languid pace.

For those who want a taste of the local scene, **Ed's Bar** (tel: 6790373), and **The Seventh Heaven** (tel: 6703188), at Martintar between Nadi International Airport and Nadi town, are the places to go. Weekends are always the busiest. Ed's Bar tends to attract a more cosmopolitan crowd whereas The Seventh Heaven is the haunt of the younger Fijian set. Friday is the busiest night and the action continues till the early hours of the morning.

Although club hours on Saturday are restricted to midnight in deference to the Sunday Observance Decree, often no one pays attention to this and the partying continues well past the hour.

Suva

As the the largest metropolitan centre in Fiji, Suva's nightlife is the most varied. As with Nadi in the west, the night scene is almost entirely confined to bars and nightclubs. The major hotels, **Holiday Inn**,

Berjaya Hotel and **Tradewinds Hotel** are best for casual drinks during the day.

O'Reilly's (tel: 3312884) is an Irish pub with a large bar and comfortable seating. It is a notch above most other establishments and attracts an interesting crowd of locals and expatriates. O'Reilly's is part of an entertainment complex and includes two restaurants, the Pizza Hut and Bad Dog Café, and the **Lucky Eddie's** nightclub and **Wolfhound** bar. Both outlets are popular with locals and visitors alike and have the advantage of being situated on Victoria Parade, Suva's main street.

The nightclubs charge a nominal admission fee and drinks are considered moderate by international standards. Friday nights tend to be jam-packed, but Lucky Eddie's is busy from midweek onwards.

Suva's nightlife offers a wide variety to suit your taste: **Birdland Bar**, Carnarvon Street (tel: 3303833), **Scandals**, 16 Bau Street (tel: 3304322) and **Shooters**, 54 Carnarvon Street (tel: 3308440).

There are two other popular watering places: **Traps** (tel: 3312922) and the **Golden Dragon** (tel: 3311018) – probably the oldest surviving nightclub in Suva – further down on Victoria Parade. Traps has a similar clientele to Lucky Eddie's.

By 11pm everyone is in place for the duration of the evening. The Golden Dragon attracts its own band of followers but it tends to be less cosmopolitan, unless you count the Taiwanese, Korean and Japanese fishermen whose boats happen to be in port for an over-haul. My recommendation would be to have a late dinner at the Pizza Hut or the Bad Dog Cafe and then check out the nightlife at Lucky Eddie's, O'Reilly's, the Wolfhound or any of the other nightspots/bars listed.

There are other places but I would not go even if you paid me to do so. Some visitors to Fiji, however, may crave a great deal more adventure and taxi drivers will be only too happy to make suggestions. Good luck!

Nightlife away from the main centres and on the smaller islands is usually restricted to the larger resorts – usually a band with amplified instruments and a makeshift disco – but even small hotels usually have a string band and a dance floor. The action really depends on the crowd, so if it's a thriving nightlife you're after, try and pick a resort that attracts a fairly young clientele.

Nightlife on resorts is low-key

Calendar of Special Events

Fiji lacks the ancient festivals and carnivals of other parts of the world, except for those celebrations introduced by its migrants like Easter, Christmas, the Hindu festival of Diwali (Festival of Lights) and the Muslim fasting month of Ramadan. Events which may have been celebrated by Fijians before the introduction of Christianity no longer exist. The only exception are ceremonies observed at the deaths of prominent chiefs and the installation of their successors. These survive in modified form and are spectacular to observe. Hotel tour desk staff usually know of such events.

Hindus perform fire walking as an act of faith. Such events are not scheduled and the date is determined by a temple priest. Once the date is set, the event is usually made known to the public. Fire walking is probably the most spectacular of events as devotees – after a 2-week period of preparation which involves abstinence from sexual intercourse and a restricted diet – gather at the nearest river or the sea for ritual cleansing. The celebrants then skewer their faces and bodies with silver pins and while in a trance, march to a temple to walk over a bed of red-hot coals.

Other festivals such as the Hibiscus

Hindu fire-walking ceremony

Festival in Suva in August, the Sugar Festival in Lautoka in September, and the Bula Festival in Nadi in July are of recent origin and no doubt will eventually become part of the fabric of the country in the near future. As dates vary from year to year, check with the **Fiji Visitors Bureau** (Suva, tel: 3302433, or Nadi, tel: 6722433) for precise dates of the festivals. The Visitors Bureau usually has a list of coming events.

JULY

Bula Festival. A week-long festival in Nadi with daily entertainment, culminating in a procession of floats, brass bands, marching contingents and beauty queens through the streets of Nadi. Festival grounds have an amusement park with carnival rides.

AUGUST

Hibiscus Festival. This is undoubtedly Suva's biggest festival. Originally begun as something for the tourists, the Hibiscus Festival is now celebrated as a week of fun for the locals. The festival held at Albert Park features a programme of nightly entertainment and culminates in a procession of floats through the streets of Suva and a grand finale at Albert Park on Saturday night when the new queen, acknowledged as Fiji's loveliest, is chosen.

SEPTEMBER

Sugar Festival. A week of fun in Lautoka in much the same vein as the Hibiscus Festival in Suva.

OCTOBER / NOVEMBER

Diwali. A traditional Hindu festival of lights in honour of the goddess Laxmi. Thousands of clay lamps are lit by Hindu devotees around homes throughout the country as people dress up in their best clothes visit each other and exchange gifts of sweets. Some of the wealthy merchants in town also festoon their homes with displays of flashing electric lights.

Held at the Mahi Devi Temple in Suva, the festival also includes fire-walking by devotees, for whom participation is an act of penance.

Ratu Bilibili Festival

NOVEMBER / DECEMBER

Ratu Bilibili Festival (chief bamboo raft festival). Held in Sigatoka, this is without doubt Fiji's most striking festival. Each year, the people of the Naitasiri province sail on large bamboo rafts, known as *bilibili,* on the Wainimala River to its confluence with the Rewa River and then onto Nausori town where they camp to raise money for their district. The fleet arrives, with more than 200 people and at the end of the day, the *bilibili* are sold to willing buyers. The people also bring fresh produce to sell. During former times when there were no roads or powered craft, much of the produce from the fertile Rewa, Wainibuka and Wainimala River valleys made its way to Nausori on bamboo *bilibili*.

PUBLIC HOLIDAYS

In addition to the variable dates for Easter and Good Friday (April/May), Diwali (October/November) and Prophet Mohammed's Birthday, the following are public holidays:

New Year's Day	January 1
Ratu Sukuna Day	May 31
Queen's Birthday	June 14
Constitution Day	July 26
Fiji Day	October 11
Christmas Day	December 25
Boxing Day	December 26

Practical Information

and generally reliable flights, although this is also the most expensive option. (See *Domestic Air* on page 85.) Check with a travel agent for current bargains. Special inter-island offers and air passes must be purchased before arrival in the country.

When leaving Fiji, all international visitors above the age of 12 must pay a F\$30 departure tax.

By Sea

Getting to Fiji by sea is difficult, except for those arriving on a cruise ship or a private yacht. Strict laws govern the entry of yachts into Fiji.

Designated ports of entry for yachtsmen sailing around the South Pacific are Suva, Lautoka, Savusavu and Levuka; other marinas include Vuda Point Marina and Musket Cove Marina on Plantation Island in the Mamanucas. Travellers planning to enter Fiji by sailing vessel must contact their Fiji High Commission well before arrival.

GETTING THERE

By Air

Fiji's two international airports are **Nadi International Airport**, on the western side of of Vitu Levi, 23km (14¼ miles) from Nadi city centre, and **Nausori International Airport**, some 23km (14¼ miles) northeast of Suva.

Both airports provide air connections to all major cities of the world, with direct flights to the USA, Canada, Australia, New Zealand, Japan and Korea. Principal international carriers include Air Pacific, Air New Zealand and Qantas Airways. Fiji's national airline, Air Pacific, flies to 16 cities in 10 countries around the Pacific.

Getting around Fiji is easy, as it is served by internal airlines with frequent

TRAVEL ESSENTIALS

When to Visit

There is no real 'season' for visiting Fiji. Australians and New Zealanders tend to favour the months of June, July, August, September and October during the course of the Southern Hemisphere winter. Visitors from the Northern Hemisphere will find Fiji most attractive from November through May when their own countries may be cold and thoughts of beautiful white-sand beaches and warm tropical south sea lagoons are inviting.

Climate and Clothing

Fiji enjoys a tropical maritime climate. There is a more pronounced wet summer season (November–April) when maximum temperatures average 30°C (86°F), although it rains throughout the year. During the drier winter months (May–October), the maximum average temperature is 26°C (79°F). It gets much cooler in the uplands of the interior of the large islands. Fiji's 'summer' and 'winter' occur in direct contrast to the Northern Hemisphere so that when it is snowing in New York, it is sunny and hot in Fiji. A cooling tradewind blows from the east-south-east for most of the year.

The mountainous nature of the principal islands has a direct effect on the climate. The prevailing east-south-east trade winds meet the mountainous barrier and deposits rain. This is great for vegetation but not so good for tourists. For this reason, most of the hotels and resorts in Fiji are located on the western or 'dry' side of the island of Viti Levu, mostly within close proximity to Nadi International Airport.

December to April is also the time when tropical cyclones from the north-west of Fiji begin trekking south and sometimes pass over the group. The cyclones usually bring winds with gusts of up to and over 100 knots near their centre and heavy rain. There is ample warning from the meteorological office and hotels and resorts are experienced in coping with problems associated with cyclones. Bad weather usually lasts no more than 24 hours. Cyclones do not necessarily occur each year. There was a period from 1967 to 1980 when Fiji recorded only one incident.

Having escaped the wrath of destructive cyclones for 20 years, Fiji was visited by two cyclones in quick succession – the relatively mild cyclone Joni in December at the close of 1992, and the more disastrous cyclone Kina which arrived on the second day of 1993. The resulting floods were the worst in more than 100 years. Tourist infrastructure, built to withstand the winds were not affected, although villages and farmers in the river valley networks received the brunt of the rains.

Visitors to Fiji need a light tropical wardrobe. Bathing suits, shorts, T-shirts and *sulus* (known also throughout the Pacific as *pareo* or *sarong*) are a must for both men and women. There are at least 10 different ways in which women can use it, even for evening wear. As the largest Christian denomination in Fiji is Wesleyan (Methodist), visitors are asked to be careful not to offend local sensibilities. Wearing bikinis and ultra-brief trunks is fine at resorts but not when visiting villages or shopping in town.

Fiji enjoys a balmy tropical climate

Gleeful Fijian youngsters

Passport and Visa

A passport valid for at least three months beyond the intended period of stay, sufficient funds and a ticket for return or onward travel are required. Entry visas are granted on arrival for a stay of 1 month for nationals of most nations. However for a few nationals, prearranged visas are required. Apply at the nearest Fiji High Commission in your respective country. Visas may be extended on application to the Department of Immigration in Suva, Lautoka or Nadi. Those wishing to stay more than six months should consult Fiji's Department of Immigration.

Vaccinations

Yellow fever and cholera vaccinations are required only for those arriving from South America or sub-Saharan Africa. Hepatitis A and B jabs are strongly advised.

Electricity

The electrical current in Fiji is 240 volts AC 50Hz. Fiji has generally three-pin power outlets identical to those in Australia and New Zealand. If your appliances are 110V, check for a 110/240V switch; if there is none you will need a voltage converter. Leading hotels and resorts generally offer universal outlets for 240V or 110V shavers, hairdryers etc.

Time Difference

Fiji is 12 hours ahead of GMT.
When it is 9am in Fiji, it is:

London	9pm	previous day
Frankfurt	10pm	previous day
New York	4pm	previous day
Los Angeles	1pm	previous day
Tokyo	6am	same day
Sydney	7am	same day
Auckland	9am	same day

GETTING ACQUAINTED

Geography

The 300 islands comprising the Republic of Fiji are scattered across more than 517,998sq km (200,000sq miles) of the South Pacific Ocean. Viti Levu with over 10,360sq km (4,000sq miles) and Vanua Levu with 5,535sq km (2,137sq miles), comprise nearly 90 percent of the total land area. Most of Viti Levu is mountainous while Vanua Levu is less so. The highest point is Mt Victoria, which is 1,323m (4,340ft) and located at the northern tip of the Nadrau plateau in Viti Levu.

The plateau has an average elevation of 900m (2,953ft) above sea level. The highest point in Vanua Levu is Mt Dikeva

Vanua Levu

which is 952m (3,123ft) high. The third largest island, Taveuni, is also geologically the youngest and owes its existence to volcanic action from Mt Uluiqalau, which at 1,241m (4,071ft) is the second highest in Fiji.

Population and People

Fiji's population is about 790,000. Indigenous Fijian people comprise 50 percent; people of Indian descent 50 percent and the balance is made up of other races. The indigenous Fijian people are among some of the friendliest in the world. The friendliness is part of the culture which regards visitors as honoured guests. Most people will smile and say hello.

If you are invited to someone's home, it is courteous to reciprocate either by buying 500g of *yaqona* (the powdered root of a plant used for ritual drinking) or food such as canned fish or corned beef. Do not go to villages wearing hats or dressed in brief shorts or swimsuits. Despite the overall courtesy and friendliness, it pays to be cautious. There are some who will take advantage of tourists (see *Shopping*, page 69).

Religion

A multi-racial, multi-cultural nation, Fiji is represented by all the major religions of the world. This is quickly obvious to the visitor who will see Christian churches, Muslim mosques and Hindu temples in the towns and countryside. The majority of Fijians are of the Wesleyan persuasion, but many other Christian denominations are represented. Sunday is observed as Sabbath with only a minimal number of shops and services operating. Visitors are welcomed to Sunday worship.

Language

Due to its British colonial heritage, Fiji is an English-speaking country, although the two major races, Fijians and Indo-Fijians both speak in their vernacular. Hotel staff are fluent in the English language. The Wesleyan missionaries who first reduced the Fijian language to a written form were faced with a number of sounds peculiar to the language. For example, a Fijian will never pronounce the letter 'd' as in day. In the Fijian language, the 'd' sound is always preceded by 'n' so that it will be pronounced 'nd' as in Nandi. This also applies to the letter 'b' which becomes 'mb'.

This is always confusing to visitors who will invariably keep mispronouncing many words such as Sigatoka, which is actually pronounced as Singatoka, Beqa, which is Bengga and the Mamanuca Islands when it should be pronounced as the Mamanutha Islands. The following tips should be helpful.

The vowels are pronounced as in the continental languages. The unusual consonant sounds are accounted as follows:

b is 'mb', as in 'remember'
c is 'th', as in 'them'
d is 'nd', as in 'candy'
j is 'ch' as in 'church'
g is 'ng' as in 'sing-along'
q is 'g', as in 'great'

Multi-ethnic Fiji

MONEY MATTERS

Currency

The Fijian dollar is the basic unit of currency. It is issued in denominations of 1, 2, 5, 10, 20 and 50 dollar notes and also as $1, 50, 20, 10, 5, 2 and 1 cent coins.

Visitors are allowed to take out currency up to the amount imported.

Credits Cards and Banks

Major credit cards are welcomed by most hotels, restaurants, shops, rental car agencies, tours, cruises and travel agents. American Express, Diners Club, VISA, JCB International and Mastercard are represented in Suva. American Express and VISA can replace lost credit cards and travellers' cheques within 24 hours.

Fiji is well represented by banking groups. These are the Australia and New Zealand group (ANZ Ltd), Bank of Baroda, Colonial National Bank, Habib Bank and Westpac Banking Corporation. All groups have head offices in Suva with agencies throughout Fiji. Automated teller services are available in major centres. ANZ runs a 24-hour banking service at Nadi International Airport's Arrival hall. Normal banking hours are from 9.30am to 3pm on Mondays through Thursdays and on Fridays till 4pm. All banks are closed on public holidays.

Business Hours

Normal business hours are 9.30am–3pm Mondays to Thursdays and till 4pm on Fridays. Most shops and commercial outlets are open five days a week as well as on Saturday mornings.

Tipping

Tipping is not encouraged in Fiji and it is left to the individual to determine whether to make a gratuity. Though tipping is not a local custom, you will find local people tipping with increasing frequency. Fijians ritually exchange gifts of food, clothing, *yaqona*, *tabua*, kerosene and money during important social occasions.

GETTING AROUND

Bus

Fiji is a small country and the cost of getting about is not great, especially if you choose to travel by local transport. This comprises buses and 'carriers' – vans and 3-ton trucks equipped with rudimentary seating that pick up and let off passengers as and where they find them. Bus companies offer express and normal services. With the express service, it is possible to go from Lautoka to Suva with stops only at Nadi, Sigatoka and Navua as well as at the hotels. Numerous air-conditioned coaches also serve the resorts and major towns on Viti Levua. Enquire at your hotel tour desk, or contact the bus companies: **Sunset Express** (tel: 3382811); **Pacific Transport** (Nadi tel: 6700044); **Sunbeam Transport** (Suva tel: 3382704); or **Fiji Express** (available through **United Touring Company Fiji**, tel: 6722811; www.atspacific.com/fiji).

Local buses fan out from the municipal markets from before daybreak to midnight between Mondays to Saturdays, and have limited schedules on Sunday. The fares vary but should cost no more than F$1 (US0.60) to most destinations in and around Suva.

If you wish to ride the bus for the fun of it, do it in Nadi, where you won't get lost and aren't as likely to be robbed.

Public bus

The older buses have canvas panel side windows and run every few minutes along the Queen's Road between Lautoka and Nadi Town, passing the airport and some hotels along the way. **Minivans** scoot along just around the corner from the Suva Municipal Market. These latter vehicles are not regulated by the government and are considered unsafe.

Taxis and Share Taxis

In Fiji, taxis come looking for you. Insist that the driver turns the meter on when you begin the ride, and if he refuses to comply, step out of the cab. Drivers will also happily make 'deals' for sightseeing and excursions for the day. As a rule of thumb, F$3 to $5 will get you to the sites of interest in the cities.

Not to be confused with unlicensed minibuses are 'share taxis' or 'rolling taxis', which pick up passengers at bus stops and are very good value for long-distance trips. Ask around at the local market bus stops if share taxis are available.

Rental Cars

Rental cars are not cheap in Fiji, due in part to the extremely high rate of import duty levied by the government on vehicles. Rental car companies are obliged to recover that cost within a 2-year operating period before selling the car. Study

Taxis are plentiful

carefully what is actually 'included' in your rental agreement. **Avis** (Nadi tel: 6722233; Suva tel: 3313833) dominates the business here, so it has the newest and best-maintained fleet. Rates start at around F$110 (US$66) per day with unlimited mileage. Add F$20 (US$12) a day for liability insurance. Drivers must be at least 21 years old (a few companies require drivers to be at least 25); your valid home driver's license will be honoured in Fiji.

Ferry

Regular ferry services ply the routes between the major islands. Deck passage is the usual way to go, though a few cabins are available on some ships on a first-come, first-served basis.

Beachcomber Cruises (tel: 3307889; www.beachcomberfiji.com) is one of the most reliable ferry companies. It runs the *Adi Savusavu* between Suva and Savusavu three times a week (about 11 hours), with extensions to Taveuni on occasion. Also in the business are **Patterson Brothers Shipping Company** (tel: 3315644) and **Consort Shipping** (tel: 3302877).

South Sea Cruises (tel: 6750500; www.ssc.com.fj) operates a large catamaran from Port Denarau through specific Mamanuca islands, while **Musket Cove** (tel: 6722488; www.musketcovefiji.com/charters) operates a smaller catamaran, which cruises between Port Denarau and Musket Cove Island Resort.

Domestic Air

Air Pacific (tel: 6720777; www.air pacific.com), the designated national airline, concentrates on overseas flights and leaves the domestic routes to **Air Fiji** (tel: 6722521; www.airfiji.net) and **Sun Air** (tel: 6723016; www.fiji.to) both fly small planes from Nadi to tourist destinations. Both have offices in the international concourse at the Nadi International Airport and on Victoria Parade in Suva. If you are going to Suva, Taveuni and Savusavu, you could save some money with a previously purchased **Air Pass** from Air Fiji. It may be worth noting that most flights between Nadi and Taveuni stop in Savusavu *en route*.

Sun Air operates domestic flights

ACCOMMODATION

There is no official rating for hotels and resorts in Fiji. Price is the only real indicator, although it would be fair to say that the most expensive is necessarily the best. At the Nadi International Airport, there is a listing of various accommodations with published rates. The Fiji Visitors Bureau at the airport will help those who have not made prior bookings. Better deals are available through your travel agent. There is no high or low season for room rates in Fiji, though specials are offered during the off-season months of February and March.

The following symbols indicate price ranges for a double standard room. All prices are subject to 12.5 percent VAT.

$	=	below $100
$$	=	F$100–$200
$$$	=	F$200–$300
$$$$	=	F$300–$700
$$$$$	=	F$700 and above

Nadi area

Located on the western side of Viti Levu, this area is home to the largest number of hotels and resorts in the country.

DOMINION INTERNATIONAL HOTEL
Tel: 6722255 Fax: 6720187
e-mail: dominionint@is.com.fj
Located along Queen's Road, close to the airport, this is an excellent base to explore the Nadi area. The rooms here are comfortable and offered at reasonable rates. *$$*

RAFFLES GATEWAY HOTEL
Tel: 6722444 Fax: 6720620
www.rafflesgateway.com
Situated opposite Nadi International Airport: most convenient for transfers. Pleasant rooms and a 24-hour courtesy bus to the airport. *$$*

SHANGRI-LA'S FIJI MOCAMBO
Tel: 6722000 Fax: 6720324
www.shangri-la.com/fiji/mocambo/en
Located near the airport with spacious grounds, the Mocambo is one of Fiji's best known hotels. Floodlight tennis and mini golf offer an alternative to a lazy day by the pool. *$$$*

SHERATON FIJI RESORT
Tel: 6750777 Fax: 6750818
www.sheraton.com/fiji
Located on Denarau Island, this modern Mediterranean-style resort has 292 ocean-view rooms with balconies overlooking both garden and sea. Four restaurants, two bars and a disco. Room rates include a buffet breakfast and complimentary non-motorised watersports. Well-run hotel with friendly staff. Large swimming pool, an adjoining 18-hole golf course and an array of daily activities. *$$$$*

SHERATON ROYAL DENARAU RESORT
Tel: 6750000 Fax: 6750259
www.sheraton.com/denarauresort

Also on Denarau Island, this resort has 273 tastefully understated rooms with strong Fijian motifs and views of either beach or gardens. Full range of facilities for dining and recreation. Good food and service. $$$$

TANOA INTERNATIONAL HOTEL
Tel: 6720277 Fax: 6720191
www.tanoahotels.com
Conveniently located just 5 minutes from the Nadi Airport, this hotel features 135 business-style rooms with views of Nadi's rolling terrain. $$$

Coral Coast

A general term to describe the resort area stretching from Momi Bay to Pacific Harbour on Viti Levu. The area up to Korotogo, 6½km (4 miles) south of Sigatoka, is situated on the 'dry' side of the island. The nearby beach is good for swimming at high tide. Sovi Bay, only 7km (4¼ miles) away, offers excellent year-round swimming.

THE CROW'S NEST
Sigatoka
Tel: 6500230 Fax: 6520354
www.crowsnestfiji.com
Private cottages with cooking facilities neatly arranged on the side of a hill overlooking the lagoon and ocean. $$

HIDEAWAY RESORT
Tel: 6500177 Fax: 6520025
www.hideawayfiji.com

On a beach in the Korolevu area, this is a fun place with a well-known surf break just beyond the barrier reef. Accommodation by the seashore in cottages set among coconut palms and flowering shrubs. Attractive pool with water slide. $$$

Sheraton Fiji Resort

NATADOLA BEACH RESORT
Natadola Beach
Tel: 6721001 Fax: 6721000
www.natadola.com
Right next to one of Fiji's best beaches along the Coral Coast, a small luxury resort with only 11 suites. Swimming pool and landscaped gardens. Childen under 16 not allowed. $$$$

NAVITI RESORT
Queens Highway, Korolevu
Tel: 6530444 Fax: 6530343
www.navitiresort.com.ff
A pleasant retreat with nice beach, pool and a nearby small island. The full range of activities are available and the staff are helpful. $$$$

OUTRIGGER ON THE LAGOON FIJI
Tel: 6500044 Fax: 6520074
www.outrigger.com/fiji
A resort offering a mix of accommodation options with spectacular views. Beautiful *bures*, grounds and pool, with views of the lagoon just beyond. $$$$

SHANGRI-LA'S FIJIAN RESORT
Yanuca
Tel: 6520155 Fax: 6500402
www.shangri-la.com/fiji/fijian/en
Set on its own private island, this resort features more than 400 rooms, an excellent beach, a 9-hole golf course, restau-

rants, bars and a shopping arcade, and a full range of activities. If you like crowds, this is the place to stay. Located only a 45-minute drive from Nadi. *$$$$*

Pacific Harbour and Beqa Island

This area has long been the playground of Suva residents. It is only 49km (30½ miles) from the city, has the longest beach in Fiji, and the nearby Beqa and Yanuca islands offer excellent fishing and diving.

BEQA LAGOON RESORT
Beqa Island
Tel: 3450100 Fax: 3450270
www.lagoonresort.com
Formerly the Marlin Bay Resort, this small award-winning hotel provides affordable rooms, friendly people, good food and amazing diving. *$$*

CENTRA RESORT
Pacific Harbour Viti Levu
Tel: 3450022 Fax: 3450262
email: centrapackharb@is.com.fj
Has 86 rooms. Excellent base for dive trips to legendary Beqa Lagoon, the nearby 'Golden Triangle' fishing waters and the famous Frigate Passage surfing waves. *$$*

Suva City

HOLIDAY INN
Victoria Parade
Tel: 3301600 Fax: 3300251
www.ichotelsgroup.com
Waterfront location within strolling dis-

tance of the heart of the city. Good service and rooms, two restaurants and pool. *$$*

HOMESTAY SUVA
265 Prince's Road
Tel: 3370395 Fax: 3370947
One of few bed-and-breakfasts in the South Pacific islands, this 1920s colonial homestay, with eight rooms, sits atop a ridge in the Tamavua suburb. Every room is comfortably furnished. *$$$*

Mamanuca Islands

The Mamanuca Islands, with their superb white-sand beaches and watersports, are just 10 minutes by air from Nadi International Airport. The airstrip on Malolo Lailai Island also serves as a pick-up point for boat transfers to other nearby resorts. A sea plane and helicopter service are available for those who wish to fly direct to their island destination. Regular passenger ferries and high-speed water taxis also service the resorts and Nadi each day.

BEACHCOMBER ISLAND RESORT
Lautoka (Tai Island)
Tel: 6661500 Fax: 6664496
www.beachcomberfiji.com
Tiny island resort filled with party-loving people. Caters to day-trippers, backpackers and the young-at-heart. Accommodation ranges from dormitories to hotel rooms and private *bures*. *$$$*

CASTAWAY ISLAND RESORT
Qalito Island
Tel: 6661233 Fax: 6665753
www.castawayfiji.com
Maintaining its Fijian-style charm despite many improvements over the years, the Castaway Island Resort has a thatched roof, and the ceilings of the *bures* are lined with genuine *masi* cloth. A very good family resort, with a helper on duty and the staff providing a wide range of activities. Couples seeking a romantic retreat should look elsewhere during holiday periods as this resort can feel rather crowded. *$$$$*

MATAMANOA ISLAND RESORT
Malolo Lailai Island
Tel: 6660511 Fax: 6661069

Samoan-style accommodation

View of Suva's Holiday Inn

www.matamanoa.com
Small, beautiful island with an attractive resort featuring *bure* accommodation, pool and a host of activities. No children. *$$$$*

MUSKET COVE RESORT
Malolo Lailai Island
Tel: 6722488 Fax: 6662633
www.musketcovefiji.com
Set on the only island in the Mamanucas with an airstrip, this beautiful resort features traditional thatched *bures* and spacious villas. *$$$*

TREASURE ISLAND RESORT
Tel: 6666999 Fax: 6666955
www.fiji-treasure.com
Located within a natural marine park, Treasure Island is the closest island resort to Nadi International Airport. Transfers are via their own cabin cruiser, and the 67 modern *bures* are all within 30 metres (90 ft) of the ocean. *$$$$*

Outer Islands

These include the islands of Naigani, Kadavu, Toberua and Wakaya.

TOBERUA ISLAND RESORT
Tel: 3302356 Fax: 3302215
www.toberua.com
This is a small exclusive retreat with 12 beachside *bures* built in a style that hon-

ours the highest chiefs. All activities and excursions inclusive in the rates, except for scuba diving and deep sea fishing. *$$$$*

VATULELE ISLAND RESORT
Tel: 6720300 Fax: 6720062
www.vatulele.com
An intimate, acclaimed, award-winning exclusive resort in a beautiful setting. A playground for the rich and famous. A minimum of 4 nights' stay is required. *$$$$$*

THE WAKAYA CLUB
Tel: 3440128 Fax: 3440406
www.wakaya.com
No Fiji hotel listing would be complete without this super-luxury resort for the wealthy and famous. Discretion and quiet are assured at daily rates that ordinary folks consider as a monthly rent. Rates include meals, bar and a diverse range of activities. *$$$$$*

Levuka

Fiji's fomer capital on Ovalau island, 10 minutes' flight from Nausori Airport.

LEVUKA HOMESTAY
Tel: 3440777
www.levukahomestay.com
Private home with four pleasant rooms with polished floors and ceiling fan. *$$*

OVALAU HOLIDAY RESORT
Tel: 3440166
www.owlfiji.com/resort
Self-contained budget bungalows set a stone's throw from the beach, about 3km (1¾ miles) from Levuka. *$*

ROYAL HOTEL
Tel: 3440024 Fax: 3440174
www.royallevuka.com
This hotel on Ovalau is Fiji's oldest, with some parts dating back to 1860. All rooms have ensuite facilities. Lovely old world charm and atmosphere. *$*

Yasawa Islands

The Yasawas form a group of spectacularly beautiful islands 40km (25 miles) north-west of Lautoka. Stunning white sand beaches, a relatively dry climate and crystal clear lagoons are the main draws of these island gems for the rich and famous.

OCTOPUS RESORT
Likuliku Bay
Tel: 6666337 Fax: 6666210
www.octopusresort.com
Aimed at the upper end of the budget market, this resort has 13 simple *bures* set on a white sandy beach offering dramatic sunsets and great snorkelling. *$$*

TURTLE ISLAND RESORT
Tel: 6722921 Fax: 6720007
www.turtlefiji.com
An exclusive luxury retreat with 14 beachside *bures*. All meals, activities and excursions inclusive in the rates, including scuba diving and deep-sea fishing. *$$$$$*

WARWICK FIJI HOTEL
Queens Road, Korolevu
Tel: 6530555 Fax: 6530010
www.warwickfiji.com
On the Coral Coast about 1½ hours from Nadi, this hotel offers many beach-oriented activities. Relatively accessible to the rest of Viti Levu. *$$$$*

YASAWA ISLAND RESORT
Tel: 6722266 Fax: 6724456
www.yasawa.com
Another luxury all-inclusive retreat, this resort on the northernmost island of the Yasawas group has 14 *bures* facing a spectacular beach. Children over 12 years accepted. *$$$$$*

Vanua Levu

Most resorts on Fiji's second largest island are clustered in the Savusavu area.

JEAN-MICHEL COUSTEAU FIJI ISLANDS RESORT
Tel: (415) 7885794 Fax: (415) 7880150
www.fijiresort.com
A very upmarket resort looking like a very luxurious old Fijian village, the Fiji Islands Resort is a water-sports paradise. Rates include meals, airport transfers and all activities except scuba diving. *$$$$*

KORO SUN RESORT
Tel: 8850352 Fax: 8850262
www.korosunresort.com
Located 13km (8 miles) east of Savusavu, on a former plantation, this newly refurbished resort has 17 *bures*, a 9-hole golf course, swimming pool, tennis courts, bush walks and ocean-side activities. *$$$*

NAMALE PLANTATION AND SPA
Tel: 8850435 Fax: 8850400
www.namalefiji.com
Set on a private peninsula facing the Koro Sea, this resort has 10 tastefully appointed *bures* with private decks and spectacular views. A wide range of activities are available, with the newest attraction here being the Spa and Sanctuary. *$$$$$*

Taveuni

Taveuni is Fiji's third largest island. Its administrative centre is at Waiyevo, but there is accommodation elsewhere and at a number of nearby islands as well.

TAVEUNI ISLAND RESORT
Tel: 8880441 Fax: 8880446

www.taveuniislandresort.com
This five-star award-winning resort offers romantic luxurious honeymoon accommodation, candle-lit dinners, smiling friendly people, diving and seclusion for just 14 guests. $$$$

COCONUT GROVE BEACHFRONT COTTAGES
Matei, Taveuni (opposite airstrip)
Tel: 8880328 Fax: 8882328
Only three cottage units. These complement the owner's very good restaurant, which overlooks the sea. No children. $$

MATANGI ISLAND RESORT
Tel: 8880260 Fax: 8880274
www.matangiisland.com
Only 10 *bures* on a 97-hectare (240-acre) privately-owned island off Taveuni's north-east coast. Owned by the Douglas family, who place special emphasis on scuba diving, deep-sea fishing and watersports. There is also a romantic treehouse hideout for honeymooners. $$$

HEALTH AND EMERGENCIES

Police

The Fiji Police Force is responsible for the maintenance of law and order and control of traffic. Police should be immediately contacted in all cases of crime and also for visa extensions when away from Suva, Nadi, Lautoka and Levuka. Telephone numbers are:

Labasa	Tel: 8881222
Lautoka	Tel: 6660222
Levuka	Tel: 3440222
Nadi	Tel: 6700222
Nausori	Tel: 3477222
Navua	Tel: 3460222
Rakiraki	Tel: 6694222
Savusavu	Tel: 8850222
Sigatoka	Tel: 6500222
Suva	Tel: 3311222
Taveuni	Tel: 8880222

Crime

Fiji has a low rate of crime against visitors but it makes sense to be careful. Theft from hotel rooms and snatch-theft in the cities are common at all hours, not just at night. Despite a strong military and police presence, muggings do occur

in the marketplaces, particularly after closing. Single women should avoid beach areas at night and refuse drinks offered to them at local bars and pubs.

Health Care

Fiji is free from malaria, yellow fever and most major diseases endemic to other tropical countries. Dengue fever is present, however, and it is indicated by a sudden onset of high fever, headache, joint and muscle pains, nausea and vomiting. A rash consisting of small red spots sometimes appears three to four days after the onset of fever. Severe complications do sometimes occur, so it is advisable to see a doctor if symptoms develop.

Travellers' diarrhoea is the leading cause of illnesses in travellers and is caused by viruses, bacteria or parasites. Make sure your food and drinking water are clean. Fresh **tap water** in Suva, Lautoka and other major towns, hotels and resorts has been treated and is, in the absence of storms, considered safe to drink, but many visitors wisely err on the safe side and drink bottled water. Some resorts use untreated artesian water for bathing, but provide drinking water separately; visitors should inquire. Certain local water holes popular for swimming have been known to seriously infect some travellers.

Health-care facilities are basic but are adequate for simple medical problems. Two major hospitals – the Lautoka Hospital in Lautoka as well as the Colonial War Memorial Hospital in Suva – provide emergency and outpatient services. In Suva, a new private hospital providing western-style medical care opened in 2000.

Crime

Nadi ambulance, tel: 6701128; hospital, tel: 6701128; police, tel: 6700222. Urgent pharmacy, Westside Drugs open Sunday 10am–noon and thereafter on call, tel: 6700310, 6780188, 6780044. Suva ambulance, tel: 3301439; hospital, tel: 3313444; police, tel: 3311222. Lautoka ambulance, tel: 6660399; police, tel: 6660222.

USEFUL ADDRESSES

Fiji Visitors Bureau
Arrivals Concourse, PO Box 9217 Nadi Airport;
Head Office: *Suite 107, Colonial Plaza, Namaka, Nadi*
Tel: 6722 433 Fax: 6720 141; and Thomson Street, Suva
Tel: 6722433 Fax: 6720141
e-mail: infodesk@bulafiji.com
www.bulafiji.com
The Thomson Street office in Suva is open extended hours and meets all international flights. In addition, there is a Tourist Police Service desk (tel: 3302433 ext 251; open Mon–Thur 8am–4.30pm, Fri 8am–4pm, Sat 8am–noon) located in this office.

For information on diving the Fiji Islands, e-mail Thomas Valentine at the Bureau: tvalentine@fijifvb.gov.fj.

Fiji Islands Hotel & Tourism Association (FIHTA)
42 Gorrie Street, PO Box 13560, Suva
Tel: 3302980 Fax: 3300331
www.fha.com.fj

Society of Fiji Travel Agents
Tel: 3302333 Fax: 3302048

Travel Agents

Victory Inland Safaris
PO Box 251, Nadi
Tel: 6700243 Fax: 6702746
e-mail: touristinfofj@connect.com.fj
www.victory.com.fj

Coral Sun Fiji
PO Box 9403, Nadi Airport, Fiji
Tel: 6723105 Fax: 6720075
e-mail: reservations@csf.com.fj

United Touring Company Fiji
PO Box 9172 Nadi Airport, Fiji

Tel: 6722811 Fax: 6720389
e-mail: fiji@utc.com.fj
www.atspacific.com/fiji

MEDIA & COMMUNICATION

Telecommunications
The international country IDD code for Fiji is 679. There are no area codes. Vodafone Fiji Ltd, a subsidiary of Telecom Fiji Ltd, operates a GSM digital mobile service. Check with your mobile network provider before travelling. Most hotels have direct dialing facilities.

Postal Services
Post offices open 8am–4pm, Monday to Friday, at all the main centres. Letters addressed to c/o The Post Office at the designated area will be held for you and delivered on proof of identity. Telegram, fax and telephone services are also available.

Media
The Fiji Times, *Daily Post* and *The Fiji Sun* are the three daily newspapers. The government, through the Fiji Broadcasting Commission, operates Radio Fiji in AM and FM frequencies: English (1089AM and 104FM); Hindi (774AM and 98FM); and Fijian (558AM). Broadcast times begin at 5am and continue until midnight. FM96, the independent commercial station, operates 24 hours a day. Television New Zealand in association with the Fiji government operates a television service in the Suva, Nadi and Lautoka areas.

RECOMMENDED READING

Biturogoiwasa, Solomoni. *My Village, My World: Everyday Life in Nadoria*, 2001.
Craig, Glen & McDonald, Bryan. *Children of the Sun*, 1996.
Katz, Richard. *The Straight Path of the Spirit: Ancestral Wisdom and Healing Traditions in Fiji*, 1999.
Lal, Brij V. *Broken Waves: A History of the Fiji Islands in the Twentieth Century*, 1992.
Nunn, Patrick. *Fiji – Beneath the Surface*, 2000.
Thornley, Andrew. *Exodus of the I Taukei, Lako Yani ni Kawa I Taukei*, 2002.

adi	A woman of chiefly rank
bete	A priest-cum-master of ceremonies
bilibili	Bamboo raft
Bula	Fijian greeting, more properly *ni sa bula vinaka*
bure	Native style house with thatched roof. Many resorts adopt this style but furnish the interior with modern facilities.
bure kalou	Ancient temple
dalo	Taro
lali	Popular wood drum
lolo	Coconut milk
love	Earth oven cooking
masi or *tapa*	Cloth made from a species of hibiscus tree specially cultivated for the purpose. The bark is stripped, soaked in water and then beaten out in varying degrees of thickness depending on the requirements of usage. Beautiful and ingenious decorations are then applied to the finished cloth. Sold in curio shops in various sizes. The National Museum has wonderful examples.
meke	Traditional communal dance/theatre
sevusevu	Necessity to give a gift
sulu	Rectangular piece of cloth
tabua	The tooth of the sperm whale presented on all important occasions, such as births, deaths, marriages, official and family requests etc. No Fijian ceremony of importance can be deemed to have taken place without the ritual presentation of *tabua*.
tanoa	Bowl for drinking *yaqona*
tapa	Cloth made from pounded bark
tavioka	Cassava (a tuber cultivated in the tropics)
turaga ni koro	Village headman, usually elected to the post. He is the chief executive of village affairs, overseeing all co-operative tasks.
vanua	Political confederation
vinaka	Thank you; good
vinaka vaka levu	Thank you very much
yaqona	The powdered root of the plant, piper mythisticum. This is mildly narcotic and is imbibed throughout Fiji by all races. As with the presentation of the *tabua*, *yaqona* (also known as *kava*) is a must on all formal and even informal occasions. Visitors wishing to see a village not on a tour schedule should always bring at least 500g of dried, unpounded roots to present to the *turaga ni koro*.

Index

ACKNOWLEDGMENTS

Photography
Cover   **Ron Dahlquist / Getty Images**
Backcover   **James Siers**
28   **Courtesy of Kula Eco Park – Fiji**
28, 29   **Courtesy of Outrigger on the Lagoon**
64, 65   **Courtesy of Rivers Fiji**
12, 13, 14/15, 16, 17 **Caines-Jannif Collections**
45   **Pat Kramer**
49T   **Topham Picture Source**
Handwriting   **V Barl**
Cover Design   **Klaus Geisler**
Cartography   **Berndtson & Berndtson**